2012 Supplement

Federal Income Taxation

SIXTH EDITION

by

PAUL R. MCDANIEL
Late Professor of Law and
James J. Freeland Eminent Scholar in Taxation
University of Florida

MARTIN J. MCMAHON, JR.
Stephen C. O'Connell Professor of Law
University of Florida

DANIEL L. SIMMONS
Professor of Law Emeritus
University of California at Davis

GREGG D. POLSKY
Willie Person Mangum Professor of Law
University of North Carolina at Chapel Hill

FOUNDATION PRESS
2012

THOMSON REUTERS

This publication was created to provide you with accurate and authoritative information concerning the subject matter covered; however, this publication was not necessarily prepared by persons licensed to practice law in a particular jurisdiction. The publisher is not engaged in rendering legal or other professional advice and this publication is not a substitute for the advice of an attorney. If you require legal or other expert advice, you should seek the services of a competent attorney or other professional.

Nothing contained herein is intended or written to be used for the purpose of 1) avoiding penalties imposed under the federal Internal Revenue Code, or 2) promoting, marketing or recommending to another party any transaction or matter addressed herein.

© 2012 by THOMSON REUTERS / FOUNDATION PRESS
    1 New York Plaza, 34th Floor
    New York, NY 10004
    Phone Toll Free (877) 888-1330
    Fax (646) 424-5201
    foundation-press.com

Printed in the United States of America

ISBN: 978-1-60930-184-2

Mat #41304180

Preface

This 2012 Supplement to Federal Income Taxation provides users of the text with materials reflecting developments in federal income taxation since July 2008 (the date as of which the materials in the text are current). This supplement is current as of June 1, 2012 and includes all significant federal income tax legislation, Treasury Regulations, judicial decisions, and Internal Revenue Service rulings promulgated after July 2008 and before June 1, 2012.

Martin J. McMahon, Jr.
Daniel L. Simmons
Gregg D. Polsky

July 1, 2012

TABLE OF CONTENTS

PREFACE iii
TABLE OF CONTENTS v
TABLE OF INTERNAL REVENUE CODE SECTIONS viii
TABLE OF TREASURY REGULATIONS ix
TABLE OF CASES AND RULINGS x

PART I INTRODUCTION TO FEDERAL INCOME TAXATION 1
CHAPTER 1 Introduction 1
Section 3. The Federal Income Tax System 1
   B. The Administrative Process 1
      (2) Administrative Interpretation Of The Tax Laws 1
   D. A Brief Survey of Income Tax Procedure 2
      (6) Interest, Penalties, And Attorneys' Fees 2
   E. The Tax Advisor 2

PART II GROSS INCOME 6
CHAPTER 3 Compensation for Services and Indirect Payments 6
Section 3. Employee Fringe Benefits 6
   A. Exclusions Based on Tax Policy and Administrative Convenience 6
CHAPTER 6 Income From the Disposition of Property 8
Section 4. Exclusion of Gains From the Sale of a Principal Residence 8
CHAPTER 7 Relationship of Basis to Income Recognition 11
Section 2. Transfers at Death: Fair Market Value Basis 11
CHAPTER 8 Taxation of Periodic Income From Capital 12
Section 1. Introduction 12
CHAPTER 9 Damage Awards and Settlements 13
Section 2. Damage Awards for Personal Injury 13
CHAPTER 10 Income From the Cancellation of Indebtedness 15
Section 1. General Principles 15
Section 2. Statutory Codification of Cancellation of Indebtedness Rules 16

PART III BUSINESS DEDUCTIONS AND CREDITS 17
CHAPTER 12 Ordinary and Necessary Business and Profit—Seeking Expenses 17
Section 5. "Public Policy" Limitations: Tax Penalties 17

CHAPTER 13 Deductible Profit-Seeking Expenses Versus Nondeductible Capital Expenditures 19
Section 1. Expenditures to Acquire or Produce Tangible Property 19
Section 2. Improvement Versus Repair or Replacement 21
Section 4. Business Investigation, Start-Up and Expansion Costs 28

CHAPTER 14 Cost Recovery Mechanisms 29
Section 1. Depreciation 29
    A. Accelerated Cost Recovery System 29
    B. Election to Expense Certain Depreciable Business Assets 30
Section 2. Statutory Amortization of Intangible Assets 30
Section 3. Expensing and Amortization Provisions 31

CHAPTER 15 Transactional Losses 32
Section 1. Business or Profit Seeking Losses 32
Section 3. Bad Debts 33

CHAPTER 17 BUSINESS TAX CREDITS 34
Section 2. General Business Credit 34
Section 3. Other Business Credits 35
Section 4. Additional Recently Enacted Credits 37

PART IV DUAL PURPOSE EXPENSES 38

CHAPTER 19 Expenses Involving Both Personal and Business Purposes 38
Section 2. Travel and Related Expenses 38
Section 3. Business Meals and Entertainment 44

PART V DEDUCTIONS AND CREDITS FOR PERSONAL LIVING EXPENSES 46

CHAPTER 21 Itemized Personal Deductions 46
Section 2. Medical Expenses 46
Section 3. Charitable Contributions 49
Section 4. State and Local Taxes 51
Section 5. Qualified Home Mortgage Interest 51

CHAPTER 22 Standard Deduction, Personal and Dependency Exemptions, and Personal Credits 53
Section 1. Personal Exemptions and the Standard Deduction 53
    B. Personal Exemptions 53
Section 2. Personal Credits 54
    A. Credits for Basic Living Expenses 54
        (1) Earned Income Credit 54
    B. Tax Credits for Personal Costs 56

CHAPTER 23 Tax Expenditures for Education.. 57

PART VI CHARACTERIZATION OF GAINS AND LOSSES................................. 58
CHAPTER 24 Capital Gains And Losses... 58
Section 1. Special Treatment of Capital Gains and Losses........................ 58
Section 2. Definition of Capital Asset.. 60
   B. Judicial Limitations on Capital Asset Classification...................... 60
CHAPTER 25 Sales of Assets Held for Use in a Trade or Business.......... 61
Section 2. Sale of an Entire Business... 61

PART VII DEFERRED RECOGNITION OF GAIN FROM PROPERTY............ 64
CHAPTER 29 Like-Kind Exchanges.. 64
Section 2. Multiparty and Deferred Exchanges 64

PART VIII TIMING OF INCOME AND DEDUCTIONS..................................... 66
CHAPTER 28 Tax Accounting Methods... 66
Section 2. The Cash Method.. 66
   A. Income Items.. 66
Section 3. The Accrual method 66
   A. Income Items.. 66
CHAPTER 29 The Annual Accounting Concept 68
Section 2. Net Operating Loss Carryover and Carryback......................... 68

PART IX TAX MOTIVATED TRANSACTIONS 69
CHAPTER 35 Statutory Limitations on Leveraged Tax Shelters............ 69
Section 2. Passive Activity Loss Limitation 69
CHAPTER 36 Economic Substance Doctrine.. 71

PART X THE TAXABLE UNIT 85
CHAPTER 37 Shifting Income Among Taxable Units 85

PART XI ALTERNATIVE MINIMUM TAX 87
CHAPTER 39 Alternative Minimum Tax for Individuals 87
Section 1. Structure of the AMT.. 87

Table of Internal Revenue Code Sections

UNITED STATES CODE
26 U.S.C.—Internal Revenue Code

Section	Page
1(g)	57
23	56
24(a)	56
24(d)	56
25A	57
23	56
24(a)	56
24(d)	56
25A	57
30D	37
32(b)	54
336	61
36A	37
38(b)	35
45Q	37
45R	35
46	2, 34
48C	34, 37
48D	37
54AA	37
54C	37
54D	37
54F	37
61(a)(12)	15
104(a)(?)	13
108(a)(1)(E)	16
108(f)	16
121	8, 9
121(b)(4)	8
1221(a)(3)(B)	49
132(f)(4)	7
132(f)(5)	6
1400U	37
1411	58
152(e)	53

UNITED STATES CODE
26 U.S.C.—Internal Revenue Code

Section	Page
162(m)(5)	17
162(m)(6)	18
165(c)(2)	32
165(h)	32
168(k)(1)(A)	29
168(m)	29
170(h)(5)(A)	51
179	30
179(d)(1)(A)(ii)	30
197	30
198	31
213	47
213(d)	46
263A	20
274(h)(7)	44
469(c)(7)	70
469(h)(2)	69, 70
1022	11
1031(a)(3)	65
1031(f)	64
4890I	48
5000A	47
5000B	48
6662	3, 4, 5, 84
6662(b)	4
6662(b)(6)	82
6662A	2, 3, 4, 5
6662A(e)(2)	82
6664(c)(2)	82
6664(d)(2)	82
6664(i)	82
6676(c)	82
6694(a)	2, 3, 4, 5
7701(o)	79, 80, 81, 82

TABLE OF TREASURY REGULATIONS

TREASURY REGULATIONS

Sec.	This Work Page
1.121-1(b)(3)	10
1.152-4	53
1.195-1(b)	28
1.1031(k)-1(b)	65
1.6662-4(d)(2)	3
1.6662-4(f)	5
1.6694-2(b)	5
1.6694-2(d)	3, 4
301.7701-15	3, 4

TEMPORARY TREASURY REGULATIONS

Sec.	This Work Page
1.162-3T(a)	22
1.162-3T(c)(1)	22
1.162-4T	22
1.263(a)-1T	20
1.263(a)-1T(d)(1)	20
1.263(a)-2T()	20
1.263(a)-2T(d)(1)	20
1.263(a)-2T(f)	21
1.263(a)-2T(f)(2)	20, 21
1.263(a)-2T(f)(2)(iv)	20
1.263(a)-3(e)	23
1.263(a)-3T	22
1.263(a)-3T(d)(1)	22
1.263(a)-3T(f)	26
1.263(a)-3T(g)	26
1.263(a)-3T(h)	23, 24, 25, 27
1.263(a)-3T(h)(4)	27
1.263(a)-3T(i)(1)	24
1.263(a)-3T(j)	24
1.263(a)-3T(j)(3)	27
1.263A-3T	20
1.469-5T(a)	70
1.469–5T(e)	69

PROPOSED TREASURY REGULATIONS

Sec.	This Work Page
§ 1.263(a)-3	22
1.469-5(e)(3)	70

TABLE OF CASES AND RULINGS

Principal cases are in bold type.
Non-principal cases are in roman type.
References are to Pages.

Boltinghouse v. Commissioner — 54
Coltec Industries, Inc. v. United States — 79
Consolidated Edison Co. of New York v. United States — 81
Domeny v. Commissioner — 14
Dominion Resources, Inc. v. United States — 27
Durden v. Commissioner — 49
Garnett v. Commissioner — 70
Gates v. Commissioner — 9
Griffin & Co. v. United States — 26
Industries, Inc. v. United States — 80
Jones v. Commissioner — 44, 49
Kaufman v. Commissioner — 50
Klamath Strategic Investment Fund v. United States — 71
Knetsch v. United States — 79
Lyseng v. Commissioner — 44
Magdalin v. Commissioner — 46
Martin Ice Cream Co. v. Commissioner — 61, 62
Mayo Foundation v. United States — 1
Melvin v. Commissioner — 15
Muskat v. United States — 62
National Federation of Independent Business v. Sebelius — 48
New Phoenix Sunrise Corporation v. Commissioner — 83
Norwalk v. Commissioner — 61
Norwest Corp. v. Commissioner — 26
Notice 2009-5 — 3, 5
O'Donnabhain v. Commissioner — 47
Ocmulgee Fields, Inc. v. Commissioner — 64

P.L.R. 201021048 — 86
Payne v. Commissioner — 15
Rendall v. Commissioner — 33
Rev. Proc. 2009-20 — 32
Rev. Proc. 2010-13 — 70
Rev. Proc. 2011-52 — 55
Rev. Rul. 2008-34 — 16
Rev. Rul. 2009-13 — 60
Rev. Rul. 2009-14 — 60
Rev. Rul. 2009-9 — 32
Rev. Rul. 94–38 — 27
Rev.Rul. 88–57 — 26
Rice's Toyota World v. Commissioner — 80
Rolfs v. Commissioner — 50
Roth Steel Tube Co. v. Commissioner — 33
Sklar v. Commissioner — 49
Solomon v. Commissioner — 62
Sophy v. Commissioner — 51
Stadnyk v. Commissioner — 13
Teruya Bros., Ltd. v, Commissioner, — 64
Thompson v. United States — 70
Trask v. Commissioner — 70
Trinity Industries, Inc. v. Commissioner — 67
United Dairy Farmers, Inc. v. United States — 27
United States v. Burke — 13
Wilbert v. Commissioner — 38

2012 Supplement

CASES AND MATERIALS

FEDERAL INCOME TAXATION

PART I

INTRODUCTION TO FEDERAL INCOME TAXATION

CHAPTER 1

INTRODUCTION

SECTION 3. THE FEDERAL INCOME TAX SYSTEM

B. THE ADMINISTRATIVE PROCESS

(2) ADMINISTRATIVE INTERPRETATION OF THE TAX LAWS

Page 31:

After the first full paragraph, insert:

In Mayo Foundation v. United States, 131 S. Ct. 704 (2011), the Supreme Court clarified the level of deference that courts are required to give Treasury regulations. Before the decision in *Mayo*, it was unclear whether Treasury regulations were evaluated under administrative law's *Chevron* standard or under a different, tax-specific standard. It was also unclear prior to *Mayo* whether the appropriate level of deference depended on whether the regulation was issued pursuant to a specific directive in a particular Code section (a so-called "legislative regulation") or pursuant to § 7805(a)'s general authority to issue tax regulations wherever necessary (an "interpretive regulation"). In *Mayo*, the Court concluded that the *Chevron* standard applies to all Treasury regulations, regardless of whether they were issued pursuant to specific directive or § 7805(a). Under step one of the *Chevron* standard, a reviewing court first determines whether Congress has directly addressed the precise question at issue. If so, Congress's determination controls. If not, the reviewing court moves on to step two, where it evaluates whether the regulation's interpretation of the statute is a reasonable one. If the interpretation is deemed reasonable, the regulation is upheld even though other reasonable interpretations might exist and even if the court would have chosen a different interpretation if it was interpreting the statute at issue without the benefit of a Treasury regulation on point.

D. A Brief Survey of Income Tax Procedure

(6) INTEREST, PENALTIES, AND ATTORNEYS' FEES

Page 46:

Replace the second sentence of the first paragraph with the following:

Section 6694(a) imposes a penalty in the amount of the greater of $1,000 or 50 percent of the income derived by the return preparer if a return or refund claim results in an understatement of liability with respect to an undisclosed position unless "there is or was substantial authority for the position." In the case of a properly disclosed position, the penalty applies if the position fails a "reasonable basis" standard. However, for positions with respect to tax shelters and reportable transactions as defined in § 6662A, i.e., certain tax shelters designated by the IRS, the preparer penalty applies "unless it is reasonable to believe that the position would more likely than not be sustained on its merits."

E. The Tax Advisor

Page 61:

After the carryover paragraph, insert:

2.   TAX RETURN PREPARER PENALTIES

Section 6694(a) imposes a penalty in the amount of the greater of $1,000 or 50 percent of the income derived by the return preparer if a return or refund claim results in an understatement of liability with respect to an undisclosed position unless "there is or was substantial authority for the position." In the case of a properly disclosed position, the penalty applies if the position fails a "reasonable basis" standard. However, for positions with respect to tax shelters and reportable transactions as defined in § 6662A (i.e., certain tax shelters designated by the IRS), the preparer penalty applies "unless it is reasonable to believe that the position would more likely than not be sustained on its merits."

Lawyers who advise clients with respect to the tax consequences of a transaction must be concerned with the tax return preparer penalties, even if they do not actually prepare a client's tax return, because the definition of a tax return preparer is quite broad. Advice on specific issues of tax law can constitute the preparation of a taxpayer's return if the advice concerns past events, is directly relevant in determining an entry on a return, and the entry relates to a "substantial" portion of the return. Treas. Reg. §§ 301.7701-15(a)(2), 301.7701-15(b). An entry that involves gross income, deductions, or amounts on the basis of which credits are determined is not substantial only if it is either (1) less than $2,000, or (2) less than $100,000 and also less than 20 percent of the gross income (or adjusted gross income if the taxpayer is an individual) shown on the return. Treas. Reg. § 301.7701-15(b)(2). Thus, advice with respect to a deduction of $25,000 claimed by a taxpayer whose adjusted gross income was $75,000, involves a substantial portion of the return.

Notice 2009-5, 2009-3 I.R.B. 309, provides that for purposes of § 6694(a) the term "substantial authority" has the meaning provided in Treas. Reg. § 1.6662-4(d)(2) of the accuracy related penalty regulations. Authority for a position is "substantial" only if the weight of authorities supporting the position relative to the weight of authorities for the contrary position is substantial. Treas. Reg. § 1.6662-4(d)(3)(i). The authorities do not need to establish that the reporting position is "more likely than not" correct, but must establish more than just a "reasonable basis" for the position. Treas. Reg. § 1.6662-4(d)(2). "Authorities" include the Code, regulations, revenue rulings and procedures, notices, judicial decisions, tax treaties and official explanations, and congressional committee reports, as well as proposed regulations, private letter rulings, technical advice memoranda, actions on decisions, information or press releases, any similar documents published by the IRS in the Internal Revenue Bulletin, and general explanations of tax legislation prepared by the staff of the Joint Committee on Taxation ("Bluebooks"). Treas. Reg. § 1.6662-4(d)(3)(iii). Secondary sources, such as law journal articles and treatises, are not considered "authority." Treas. Reg. § 1.6662-4(d)(3)(ii). Authorities must be weighed as a court would in deciding the proper treatment of the item.

The regulations provide important guidance regarding the standards for complying with § 6694. Under Treas. Reg. § 1.6694-2(d)(3)(i), if a signing tax return preparer (as defined in Treas. Reg. § 301.7701-15(b)(1)) believes that there is a reasonable basis for a position (other than a position with respect to a tax shelter or a reportable transaction to which § 6662A applies), but the position does not meet the substantial authority standard, the requirements of § 6694 can be satisfied by disclosure in one of three ways.

(1) The position may be disclosed on a properly completed and filed Form 8275, Disclosure Statement, or Form 8275-R, Regulation Disclosure Statement, as appropriate, or on the tax return in accordance with the annual revenue procedure.

(2) The tax return preparer provides the taxpayer with a prepared tax return that includes the appropriate disclosure.

(3) For tax returns or claims for refund that are subject to penalties other than the accuracy-related penalty for substantial understatements under §§ 6662(b)(2) and (d), the tax return preparer advises the taxpayer of the penalty standards applicable to the taxpayer under § 6662 and contemporaneously documents in his files that this advice was provided. This third rule addresses situations in which the penalty standard applicable to the taxpayer is based on compliance with requirements other than disclosure on the return.

In the case of a nonsigning tax return preparer (as defined in Treas. Reg. § 301.7701-15(b)(2), Treas. Reg. §1.6694-2(d)(3)(ii) provides that a position (other than a position with respect to a tax shelter or a reportable transaction to which § 6662A applies) for which there is a reasonable basis but which does not satisfy the substantial authority standard may be disclosed in one of three ways.

(1) The position may be disclosed on a properly completed and filed Form 8275, Disclosure Statement, or Form 8275-R, Regulation Disclosure Statement, as appropriate, or on the tax return in accordance with the annual revenue procedure.

(2) The nonsigning tax return preparer advises the taxpayer of all opportunities to avoid penalties under § 6662 that could apply to the position and advises the taxpayer of the standards for disclosure to the extent applicable, and contemporaneously documents in his files that this advice was provided.

(3) If a nonsigning tax return preparer provides advice to another tax return provider with respect to the position, the nonsigning tax return preparer advises the other tax return preparer that disclosure under § 6694(a) may be required, and contemporaneously documents in his files that this advice was provided.

For both signing and nonsigning return preparers, if a position for which there is a "reasonable basis" but for which there is not "substantial authority" is not disclosed on or with the return, each return position must be addressed by the tax return preparer. Treas. Reg. § 1.6694-2(d)(3)(iii). The advice to the taxpayer with respect to each position must be particular to the individual taxpayer's facts, and the tax return preparer must contemporaneously document that this advice was given. Treas. Reg. § 1.6694-2(d)(3)(iii).

Treas. Reg. § 1.6694-2(e) provides that the § 6694 penalty can be avoided if, considering all the facts and circumstances, the preparer demonstrates that the understatement was due to reasonable cause and that the tax return preparer acted in good faith.

If the return position was with respect to a tax shelter or a § 6662A reportable transaction, and the preparer knew, or reasonably should have known, of the position, the § 6694 penalty applies if it was not reasonable to believe that the position would more likely than not be sustained on its merits. Treas. Reg. §§ 1.6694-2(a)(1)(ii), 1.6694-2(a). It is "reasonable to believe that a position would more likely than not be sustained on its merits" if the tax return preparer analyzes the pertinent facts and authorities and, in reliance upon that analysis, reasonably concludes in good faith that the position has a greater than 50 percent likelihood of being sustained on its merits. Treas. Reg. § 1.6694-2(b). Whether this standard has been met is based upon all the facts and circumstances, including the return preparer's due diligence. The advisor's conclusion cannot be based on unreasonable factual or legal assumptions and the advisor must not unreasonably rely on the representations, statements, findings, or agreements of the taxpayer or any other person. The possibility that the position will not be challenged by the IRS, either because the taxpayer's return may not be audited or the issue may not be raised on audit, cannot be considered.

Notice 2009-5, 2009-3 I.R.B. 309, provides temporary guidance concerning tax shelters. Until additional guidance is issued, for purposes of § 6694(a), a position with respect to a tax shelter (as defined in § 6662(d)(2)(C)(ii)) will not be deemed to be an "unreasonable position" if there is substantial authority for the position and the tax return preparer advises the taxpayer of the penalty standards that would be applicable if the transaction is deemed to have a significant purpose of tax avoidance or evasion. The taxpayer must be advised that if the position has such a significant purpose, (1) there must be at least substantial authority for the position, (2) the taxpayer must possess a reasonable belief that the tax treatment is more likely than not the proper treatment to avoid a penalty under § 6662(d), and (3) disclosure pursuant to Reg. § 1.6662-4(f) will not protect the taxpayer from assessment of an accuracy related penalty if § 6662(d)(2)(C) applies to the position. The advice provided by the tax return preparer must be contemporaneously documented in the tax return preparer's files. Similarly, advice provided by a nonsigning tax return preparer to another tax return preparer with respect to a tax shelter will not be deemed to be an "unreasonable position" if there is substantial authority for the position and the tax return preparer provides a statement about the penalty standards applicable to the preparer under § 6694 and contemporaneously documents the provision of the statement. The interim penalty compliance rules provided by Notice 2009-5 do not apply to positions with respect to § 6662A transactions (reportable transactions with a significant purpose of Federal tax avoidance and evasion or listed transactions).

PART II

GROSS INCOME

CHAPTER 3

COMPENSATION FOR SERVICES AND INDIRECT PAYMENTS

SECTION 3. EMPLOYEE FRINGE BENEFITS

A. EXCLUSIONS BASED ON TAX POLICY AND ADMINISTRATIVE CONVENIENCE

Page 112:

In the third full paragraph, delete the seventh and eighth sentences and insert after the end of the paragraph:

Thinking "green," Congress has expanded the transportation fringe benefit to include any "qualified bicycle commuting reimbursement," which includes employer reimbursements "for the purchase of a bicycle and bicycle improvements, repair, and storage, if such bicycle is regularly used for travel between the employee's residence and place of employment." I.R.C. § 132(f)(5)(F)(i). The maximum amount of bicycle commuting reimbursements that may be excluded in any taxable year is $240. I.R.C. § 132(f)(5)(F)(ii).

Section 132(f)(4) provides that if employees are given a choice of qualified transportation fringes or cash and an employee accepts the qualified transportation fringe, no amount will be includable as a result of the employee having this choice. However, this tax-free choice is not available for qualified bicycle commuting reimbursements.

CHAPTER 6

INCOME FROM THE DISPOSITION OF PROPERTY

SECTION 4. EXCLUSION OF GAINS FROM THE SALE OF A PRINCIPAL RESIDENCE

Page 230:

At the end of the second full paragraph, insert:

1.4. *Limitation on Excluded Gains From Converted Property*

In the Housing Assistance Tax Act of 2008, Congress limited the amount of gain that could be excluded under § 121 with respect to rental properties and vacation homes that are subsequently converted to principal residences. New § 121(b)(4) provides that gain on the sale of a personal residence is not excluded from gross income to the extent that the gain is allocable to periods of "nonqualified use" of the residence. In general, periods of nonqualified use include periods in which the property is not used as a principal residence of the taxpayer (or of the taxpayer's current or former spouse). However, (1) use prior to January 1, 2009 is not treated as nonqualified use, (2) use after the last date that the taxpayer used the property as a principal residence is not treated as a nonqualified use, (3) use while the taxpayer is on certain official governmental extended duty (e.g., military) is not nonqualified use, and (4) use during any other period of temporary absence (for up to an aggregate period of two years) is not nonqualified use if the absence is due to specified unforeseen circumstances. The amount of gain not excluded by reason of § 121(b)(4) is determined by allocating the total gain to periods of nonqualified use based on the ratio that the aggregate period of nonqualified bears to the total time the taxpayer owned the property. For example, assume that a taxpayer buys a property on January 1, 2009, for $500,000, and uses it exclusively as a vacation home for 12 years. On January 1, 2021, the taxpayer converts the property to his principal residence. On January 1, 2024, the taxpayer sells the property for $800,000. The twelve years of vacation use is a period of nonqualified use that is eighty percent of the taxpayer's fifteen-year period of ownership; accordingly, eighty percent ($240,000) of the $300,000 total gain is allocated to the period of nonqualified use and is therefore not eligible for exclusion under § 121. The remaining $60,000 of gain is excluded from gross income.

Page 232:

After the first full paragraph, insert:

 In Gates v. Commissioner, 135 T.C. 1 (2010), the Tax Court addressed the question of whether the taxpayer was required actually to have physically resided in the particular dwelling unit that was sold to be eligible to claim the § 121 exclusion. In that case, the married taxpayers had owned and occupied a house as a principal residence for at least two years. They wanted to enlarge and remodel the house but were advised by an architect that more stringent building and permit restrictions had been enacted since the house was built. In 1999, rather than remodel the house, they completely demolished it and constructed a new house on the property. The taxpayers never occupied the new house, and subsequently sold it, realizing a gain of over $500,000. They claimed that $500,000 of the gain was excludable under § 121, but the IRS denied the exclusion because they had never occupied the new structure and it thus never was their "principal residence," even though it occupied land on which had been located their former principal residence. The IRS's argument interpreted "the term 'property' [in § 121(a)] to mean, or at least include, a dwelling that was owned and occupied by the taxpayer as his "principal residence" for at least 2 of the 5 years immediately preceding the sale." The taxpayers argued that the term "property" in § 121(a) includes not only the dwelling but also the land on which the dwelling is situated, and that the requirements of §121(a) are satisfied if the taxpayer lived in any dwelling on the property for the required 2-year period, even if that dwelling is not the dwelling that was sold. Under the taxpayer's theory, because they used the original house and the land on which it was situated as their principal residence for the required term, the land and building that were sold qualified as their principal residence. Finding that the statute did not define the terms "property" and "principal residence," the majority of the Tax Court examined the background of §121, including its statutory predecessors, former § 1034 and its predecessor in the 1939 Code, and held that:

> Congress intended the term "principal residence" to mean the primary dwelling or house that a taxpayer occupied as his principal residence. ... Although a principal residence may include land surrounding the dwelling, the legislative history supports a conclusion that Congress intended the section 121 exclusion to apply only if the dwelling the

taxpayer sells was actually used as his principal residence for the period required by section 121(a).

In a footnote the court's opinion noted that Reg. § 1.121-1(b)(3), as currently in effect, allows gain from the sale of land alone to qualify under § 121 if the taxpayer also sells "a 'dwelling unit' that meets the requirements under sec. 121 within 2 years before or after the sale of the land." The dissenting opinion would have allowed the exclusion, treating the demolition and reconstruction no differently from a renovation. It expressed concern that drawing the line between a "remodeling," which presumably would not start the 2-year clock running anew and a "rebuilding," which under the majority opinion does start the 2-year clock running anew is a difficult line to draw, asking rhetorically "is there some level of remodeling that does (1) terminate the use of the home as the taxpayer's principal residence and (2) set the temporal clock to zero?"

CHAPTER 7

RELATIONSHIP OF BASIS TO INCOME RECOGNITION

Section 2. Transfers at Death: Fair Market Value Basis

Page 240:

Delete the first full paragraph. Section 1022 is no longer applicable.

Pages 242-245:

Delete part 4, "MODIFIED TRANSFERRED BASIS AT DEATH STARTING IN 2010".

CHAPTER 8

TAXATION OF PERIODIC INCOME FROM CAPITAL

SECTION 1. INTRODUCTION

Page 261:

After the second full paragraph add:

Beginning in 2013, investment income earned by certain higher-income individuals will be subject to an additional 3.8 percent income tax surtax under § 1411. While the tax imposed by new § 1411 is an employment tax provision, it operates as income tax surtax. The surtax applies to the lesser of (1) net investment income and (2) the excess of adjusted gross income over a threshold amount. The threshold amount is $250,000 for spouses filing a joint return and $200,000 for single taxpayers. The surtax was enacted as part of the Patient Protection and Affordable Care Act of 2010 to help fund the subsidies provided to lower-income individuals to purchase health insurance.

CHAPTER 9

DAMAGE AWARDS AND SETTLEMENTS

SECTION 2. DAMAGE AWARDS FOR PERSONAL INJURY

Page 313:

Replace the first full paragraph with the following:

Recently promulgated Treas. Reg. § 1.104-1(c) eliminates the requirement in the former regulations that to be excludable under § 104(a)(2) damages must be "based upon tort or tort type rights." This change allows damages for physical injuries to qualify for exclusion under § 104(a)(2) even though the injury giving rise to the damages is not defined as a tort under state or common law. The Treasury Department promulgated the change because of its concern that the Supreme Court's interpretation of the tort type rights test in United States v. Burke, 504 U.S. 229 (1992), limiting the § 104(a)(2) exclusion to damages for personal injuries for which the full range of tort-type remedies is available, could preclude an exclusion under § 104(a)(2) for redress of physical personal injuries under a "no-fault" statute that does not provide traditional tort-type remedies.

At the end of the second full paragraph, add:

Stadnyk v. Commissioner, T.C. Memo. 2008-289 (2008), aff'd, 105 A.F.T.R.2d 2010-1130 (6th Cir. 2010), held that damages received on account of false imprisonment were not excludable under § 104(a)(2), even though the taxpayer was detained, handcuffed, and searched, because she suffered no physical harm. Instead, the court determined, the taxpayer received the damages on account of her emotional distress, mortification, humiliation, mental anguish, and reputational harm.

At the beginning of the third full paragraph, insert:

Treas. Reg. § 1.104-1(c) provides, consistent with the legislative history, that emotional distress is not considered a physical injury or physical sickness. However, the regulation also provides that damages for emotional distress that are attributable to a physical injury or physical sickness are excludable under

§ 104(a)(2). Cases that predated the regulation were consistent with this approach.

Page 316:

After the second full paragraph, insert:

In Domeny v. Commissioner, T.C. Memo. 2010-009, the taxpayer received approximately $33,000 from her former employer to settle a claim for wrongful termination of employment and violations of various civil rights statutes (of which $8,000 was paid to her lawyer). The employer issued her a Form W-2 that reflected approximately $8,000 as employee compensation, and $17,000 to the taxpayer that was shown on a Form 1099-MISC as "nonemployee compensation." The $8,000 paid directly to the taxpayer was includable wage compensation, and the remaining amount was excludable under § 104(a)(2) as damages for physical injuries attributable to exacerbation of the employee's multiple sclerosis caused by a hostile work environment. The employer's intent in settling the claim was evidenced by the issuance of separate checks and different information returns, and these facts indicated that the employer intended the amount in excess of wages due to be in settlement of tort claims for physical injuries attributable to the exacerbation of the multiple sclerosis. Likewise, in Parkinson v. Commissioner, T.C. Memo. 2010-142, the Tax Court determined that one-half of the amount received by the taxpayer in settlement of a claim for intentional infliction of emotional distress was excludable under § 104(a)(2) because the payor intended that portion to be compensation for a heart attack suffered as a result of the emotional distress. The court reasoned that "a heart attack and its physical aftereffects constitute physical injury or sickness rather than mere subjective sensations or symptoms of emotional distress." The other one-half of the settlement was not excludible because it represented compensation for emotional distress.

CHAPTER 10

INCOME FROM THE CANCELLATION OF INDEBTEDNESS

SECTION 1. GENERAL PRINCIPLES

Page 324:

At the end of the carryover paragraph, add:

The Tax Court's decision in Payne was affirmed, 357 Fed. Appx. 734 (8th Cir. 2009).

Page 327:

After the carryover paragraph, insert:

3. EFFECT OF TRANSACTION COSTS ON AMOUNT OF CANCELLATION OF DEBT INCOME

Unless the taxpayer is in a trade or business or the debt relates to a transaction entered into for profit, transaction costs incurred to secure the cancellation of the debt are neither deductible nor an offset against the amount of the debt cancellation that must be included under § 61(a)(12). In Melvin v. Commissioner, T.C. Memo. 2009-199, the taxpayers owed a bank $13,084 on a consumer credit cards. The bank agreed to accept $4,579 to settle the debt, and the taxpayers paid a third party 25 percent of the $8,505 savings, or $2,126 to negotiate the compromise. The court rejected the taxpayer's argument that under § 61(a)(12) itself only the net benefit of the debt cancellation, i.e., $6,379, was includable in gross income.

SECTION 2. STATUTORY CODIFICATION OF CANCELLATION OF INDEBTEDNESS RULES

Page 332:

After the first sentence of the first paragraph, add:

The Emergency Economic Stabilization Act of 2008 extended the qualified principal residence indebtedness rule in § 108(a)(1)(E) through December 31, 2012.

After the first paragraph, add:

7. DISCHARGE OF STUDENT LOANS

Section 108(f) provides an exclusion for gross income resulting from the discharge (in whole or in part) of any student loan (or any loan made to refinance a student loan) if the discharge was pursuant to a loan provision that provided for the discharge if the borrower worked for a certain period of time in certain professions for any of a broad class of employers. Loan repayment assistance programs (LRAP) now provided by law schools are often designed to qualify for exclusion under this provision. These programs make loans to students to allow them to make scheduled payments on their student loans; the LRAP loans are subsequently forgiven by the law school if the student works for specified periods of time for the government or for public interest organizations. See Rev. Rul. 2008-34, 2008-2 C.B. 76 (analyzing a typical LRAP loan and concluding that its forgiveness would qualify under § 108(f)).

PART III

BUSINESS DEDUCTIONS AND CREDITS

CHAPTER 12

ORDINARY AND NECESSARY BUSINESS AND PROFIT—SEEKING EXPENSES

SECTION 5. "PUBLIC POLICY" LIMITATIONS: TAX PENALTIES

Page 415:

After the carryover paragraph, add:

Congress enacted bright-line compensation deduction limits applicable to certain types of corporations. As part of the Emergency Economic Stabilization Act of 2008, Congress added paragraph (5) of § 162(m), which disallows compensation deductions that would otherwise be available to certain businesses that received financial assistance from the federal government under the Troubled Asset Relief Program (TARP). Under this provision, TARP beneficiaries generally may not deduct annual compensation paid to the five most senior executives in excess of $500,000. Unlike the general § 162(m) rule, there is no carve-out for performance-based compensation. In addition, § 162(m)(5) attempts to prevent TARP beneficiaries from circumventing the disallowance by increasing an executive's deferred compensation, which is a common strategy to avoid the general § 162(m) rule.

The Patient Protection and Affordable Care Act of 2010 extended these special rules for TARP beneficiaries to certain health insurance providers. New § 162(m)(6) is similar in many respects to (m)(5). They both limit compensation deductions to the first $500,000 of compensation, without any carve-out for performance-based compensation, and they both contain rules to prevent taxpayers from using deferred compensation to circumvent the disallowance. However, while (m)(5) applies only to compensation paid to the most senior executives, (m)(6) applies to all persons who provide services to the health insurance provider, regardless of whether the person is an employee or independent contractor. The new provision will not become effective until 2013. The theory behind the new provision appears to be that, because the new health care law requires individuals to purchase health insurance policies, health insurance providers will receive a windfall by virtue of the increased demand for insurance. If the provision is effective in reducing the amount of compensation paid to service providers, then it would impede ability of those service providers to capture that windfall.

Chapter 13

Deductible Profit-Seeking Expenses Versus Nondeductible Capital Expenditures

Section 1. Expenditures to Acquire or Produce Tangible Property

Page 418:

Change the citations to the Regulations to the following:

REGULATIONS: Section 1.212-1(k), (n)
TEMPORARY REGULATIONS: Sections 1.263(a)-1T, -2T

Page 421:

In the second full paragraph, replace the last three sentences with the following:

The 2008 proposed regulations were thereafter replaced with temporary regulations that became effective on January 1, 2012.

Page 422:

Replace the last the two sentences of the carryover paragraph from the previous page with the following:

The 2012 temporary regulations allow taxpayers who obtain audited financial statements for non-tax purposes to immediately deduct the cost of otherwise capitalized expenditures if (i) such cost is treated as an expense on the financial statements and (ii) the aggregate amount of such costs for the taxable year are less than or equal to the greater of .1 percent of the taxpayer's gross receipts (as determined for tax purposes) for such year or 2 percent of the taxpayer's total depreciation and amortization expense (as determined for financial accounting purposes) for such year. Treas. Reg. § 1.263(a)-2T(g).

Page 423:

Replace the last sentence of the carryover paragraph from the previous page with the following:

Apart from § 263A, the 2012 temporary regulations, which generally require capitalization of expenditures incurred to faciliate the acquisition or production of tangible property, allow the immediate deduction of employee compensation and overhead that are incurred in connection with the acquistion or production of tangible property. The temporary regulations accomplish this result by classifying employee compensation and overhead as costs that are deemed to not facilitate the acqusition or production of tangible property. Temp. Reg. § 1.263(a)-2T(f)(2)(iv).

Page 424:

Replace the fifth sentence of the second full paragraph with the following:

Capitalization of expenditures to acquire, improve, or restore tangible property that is not subject to § 263A is governed by the 2012 temporary regulations. See Temp. Reg. §1.263(a)-1T, 2T, and 3T.

Page 426:

Replace the first the two sentences of the second full paragraph with the following:

The cost of acquiring an asset that will not be consumed or depleted during the current period is a capital expenditure in its entirety. Temp. Reg. § 1.263(a)-2T(d)(1). The cost of disposing of an asset is similarly a capital cost that reduces gain (or increases loss) on the disposition. Temp. Reg. § 1.263(a)-1T(d)(1).

Page 427:

Replace the second full paragraph with the following:

Temp. Reg. § 1.263(a)-2T(f) requires capitalization of expenses incurred to faciliate the acquisition or production of property. Facilitative costs that must be capitalized include amounts paid in the process of investigating or pursuing the acquisition of property including transporting the property, determining value, negotiating the acquisition and obtaining tax advice regarding the acquisition, application fees, bidding costs, document review, title review, securing regulatory approval, finders' fees and brokers' commissions, and architectural, engineering, and other inspections. Temp. Reg. § 1.263(a)-2T(f)(2)(i), (ii). With respect to real property, expenses that facilitate an acquisition do not include investigation expenses incurred "in the process of determining whether to acquire real property and which real property to acquire." Temp. Reg. § 1.263(a)-2T(f)(2)(iii). In addition, facilitative costs in acquiring property (whether real or personal) generally do not include employee compensation and overhead costs. Temp. Reg. § 1.263(a)-2T(f)(2)(iv).

Page 428:

Replace the first sentence of the first full paragraph with the following:

Under the origin-of-the-claim test of *Woodward*, page 426, litigation and related expenses to defend or perfect title to property are capital expenditures. Temp. Regs. §§ 1.212-1(k) and 1.263-2T(e).

Replace the carryover paragraph to the following page with the following:

Temp. Reg. § 1.263(a)-2T(e) expressly provides that amounts paid to defend or perfect title to real or personal property must be capitalized. As examples, the regulation indicates that amounts paid to contest condemnation or to challenge a local agency decision to establish a building line across property owned by the taxpayer are capital expenditures. Temp. Reg. § 1.263(a)-2T(e)(2), Exs. (1) & (3). On the other hand, expenses incurred to invalidate a local ordinance that would prohibit the taxpayer's on-going business of operating a quarry on the taxpayer's land are incurred to protect the taxpayer's business activities and are not required to be capitalized. Temp. Reg. § 1.263(a)-2T(e)(2), Ex. (2).

SECTION 2. IMPROVEMENT VERSUS REPAIR OR REPLACEMENT

Page 430:

Delete the citation to the Prop. Reg. § 1.263(a)-3, and insert:
TEMPORARY REGULATIONS: Sections 1.162-4T; 1.263(a)-3T

Page 436:

Replace the text in section 1.1. *In General,* **with the following:**

Traditionally, the tax law distinguished between costs of incidental repairs and maintenance of property, which were currently deductible, and costs that materially added to the value of the property or substantially prolonged its useful life, which were nondeductible capital expenditures. Temporary regulations that became effective in 2012 modified this approach, providing that the basic test for distinguishing capital expenditures from repairs is whether the expenditure "improves" a unit of property. An expenditure improves a unit of property if the expenditure either (1) results in a "betterment" to the unit of property, (2) restores the property, or (3) adapts the property to a new or different use. Temp. Reg. § 1.263(a)-3T(d)(1), (h), (i) and (j). Any expenditure that is not required to be capitalized under Temp. Reg. § 1.263(a)-3T is considered a deductible repair. Temp. Reg. § 1.162-4T. In addition, amounts expended for "routine maintenance" are currently deductible. Routine maintenance is defined in the temporary regulations as "the recurring activities that a taxpayer expects to perform as a result of the taxpayer's use of the unit of property to keep the unit of property in its ordinarily efficient operating condition." Temp. Reg. § 1.263(a)-3T(e)(1).

Page 438-444:

Replace sections 1.3, 2, and 3 with the following:

1.3 *Temporary Regulations*

The 2012 Temporary regulations abandon the prior judicial and regulatory focus on material increase in value and focus instead on whether an expenditure results in an "improvement" to a unit of property in the form of a "betterment", restoration, or adaptation to a different use. Temp. Reg. § 1.263(a)-3T(d)(1). Nonetheless, the temporary regulations, through numerous examples, adopt many of the results of prior judicial and regulatory decisions.

1.3.1. *Unit of Property*

The temporary regulations look to improvements in a "unit of property" to determine whether an expenditure must be capitalized. Tangible property that is not a unit of property is treated as "materials and supplies," the cost of which is deductible when the materials or supplies are used or consumed (or in the case of incidental material and supplies, when purchased). Temp. Reg. § 1.162-3T(a), (c)(1). Materials and supplies also include a unit of property that has an economic useful life of 12-months or less or that costs less than $100. Temp. Reg. § 1.162-3T(c)(1)(iii) & (iv). This provision is a de minimis standard that allows a deduction for short-lived property, even though the property may be used by the taxpayer over two taxable years.

The temporary regulations define a unit of property as including all of the components of real or personal property that are functionally interdependent. Temp. Reg. § 1.263(a)-3(e). Generally, components of a unit of property are functionally interdependent if the placing in service of one component is dependent on the placing in service of the other component. Temp. Reg. § 1.263(a)-3T(e)(3). However, components are treated as separate units of property if each component is recorded on the books as having a different economic useful life or each component is included in a different class of property for purposes of MACRS depreciation. Temp. Reg. § 1.263(a)-3T(e)(5)(i). Thus, for example, although a truck trailer and its tires are functionally interdependent, if the trailer and the tires are recorded on the books with different economic useful lives, the trailer and tires are treated as separate units of property. Temp. Reg. § 1.263(a)-3T(e)(6), Ex. (16). A building and its structural components are treated as a unit of property. Temp. Reg. § 1.263(a)-3T(e)(2)(i). A special rule for "plant property"—a functionally integrated collection of equipment and machinery used to perform an industrial process—separates equipment and machinery into one component or group of components that each perform a discrete and major function or operation. Temp. Reg. § 1.263(a)-3T(e)(3)(ii).

1.3.2. *Capitalization of "Betterments" to a Unit of Property.*

An expenditure is classified as a "betterment" and required to be capitalized if, under the facts and circumstances, the expenditure ameliorates a material condition or defect that existed prior to the taxpayer's acquisition of the property or arose during production (whether or not the taxpayer was aware of the defect prior to placing the property in service), results in a material addition to the unit of property, or results in a material increase in capacity, strength or quality of the unit of property or the output of the unit of property. Temp. Reg. § 1.263(a)-3T(h)(1). The taxpayer's installation of its concrete lining in Midland Empire Packing Company, page 430 of the text, would not be treated as a betterment because the expenditure did "not result in a material addition or material increase in capacity, productivity, efficiency, strength or quality of the building structure or its output compared to the condition of the structure prior to the seepage of the oil." Temp. Reg. § 1.263(a)-3T(h)(4), Ex. (12). The example adds that under Temp. Reg. § 1.263(a)-3(f)(2), the fact that the taxpayer added the concrete liner to comply with regulatory requirements is not relevant. The temporary regulations also confirm the result in Mt. Morris Drive-in Theater Company v. Commissioner, page 433, because the expenditure was incurred to correct a condition that existed prior to the taxpayer's development of the drive-in theater. See, e.g., Temp. Reg. § 1.263(a)-3T(h)(4), Ex. (5)(ii).

The temporary regulations address the question raised by the contrast between *Oberman* and *Connally,* namely whether in determining that an expenditure materially adds to the value of property, value is to be measured by looking to the situation prior to the time the expenditure is made or prior to the time the condition necessitating the expenditure arose. Temp. Reg. § 1.263(a)-3T(h)(3)(iii) provides that in cases where a particular event requires an expenditure, the appropriate comparison is between the condition of the property after the expenditure with the condition of the property immediately prior to the circumstances necessitating the expenditure. This formulation suggests that raising the entry level in *Connally* because of the street level change would be deductible. The temporary regulations also add that where an expenditure is made to correct normal wear and tear to a unit of property, the appropriate comparison is to the condition of the unit of property after the last time the taxpayer corrected the effects of normal wear and tear. Temp. Reg. § 1.263(a)-3(h)(3)(iii)(B).

1.3.3. *Capitalization of Restoration Expenditures*

The temporary regulations require capitalization of an expenditure to restore a unit of property. Temp. Reg. § 1.263(a)-3T(i)(1). Restoration includes replacement of a component of a unit of property where the taxpayer has recovered its basis in the component through a loss deduction for the component, in the realization of gain or loss on a sale or exchange of the component, or through a basis adjustment attributable to a casualty loss. In addition, restoration includes an expenditure that returns a non-functional unit of property that is in a state of disrepair to its ordinarily efficient operating condition, rebuilds a unit of property to a like-new condition after the end of its economic useful life, or replaces a major component or substantial structural part of a unit of property. An expenditure that rebuilds a unit of property to a like-new condition before the end of its economic useful life, or is paid during the recovery period of the property under § 168(c), is not required to be capitalized. Temp. Reg. § 1.263(a)-3T(i)(1)(v) & (i)(5), Ex.(6).

1.3.4. *Expenditures to Adapt Property to a New or Different Use.*

Expenditures to adapt a unit of property to new or different use that is not consistent with the taxpayer's use of the property when first placed in service would be required to be capitalized. Temp. Reg. § 1.263(a)-3T(j)(1). The temporary regulations warn that an expenditure that is not required to be capitalized as adapting a unit of property to a new use may still be required to be capitalized under another provision of the temporary regulations. Temp. Reg. § 1.263(a)-3T(j)(3). Under the temporary regulations, expenditures incurred to remodel a manufacturing facility to provide a showroom for the taxpayer's business must be capitalized because the property is converted to a new use. Temp. Reg. § 1.263(a)-3T(j)(3), Ex. (1). On the other hand, expenses to combine three retail spaces into a single larger space in a building that is rented to several retail tenants is not required to be capitalized as an adaptation to a new use because the building continues to be used for rental to retail tenants. Temp. Reg. § 1.263(a)-3T(j)(1), Ex. (2). Similarly, expenditures to renovate a building by painting the walls and refinish floors in preparation of selling the building are not incurred to adapt the building to a different use. Temp. Reg. § 1.263(a)-3T(j)(2), Ex. (3).

2. ROUTINE MAINTENANCE

As noted in *Oberman,* page 437 of the text, a properly performed repair adds value, which may be beneficial over a number of taxable years. In Ingram Industries, Inc. v. Commissioner, T.C. Memo. 2000–323, expenses for periodic maintenance of inland barge towboat engines were deductible as repairs and were not capital expenditures because the engines were not separate property from the boats themselves, the work was not the equivalent of completely rebuilding or overhauling the engines, and there was no way to measure any increment in value of a boat resulting from the maintenance. The temporary regulations adopt the result in *Ingram* with a safe harbor for routine maintenance expenditures, which is defined as recurring activities that the taxpayer expects to perform to keep the property in its ordinary operating condition. Temp. Reg. § 1.263(a)-3T(g)(1) & (5), Ex. (8). However, expenditures that result in a betterment to the unit of property, for example, engine upgrades in the course of periodic maintenance that increase the power of the towboat, require capitalization. Temp. Reg. § 1.263(a)-3T(g)(5), Ex. (9).

The safe harbor for routine maintenance encompasses only maintenance performed as a result of the taxpayer's use of a unit of property. Thus, if the taxpayer acquires a fully operational machine that is near the end of its scheduled maintenance period, scheduled periodic maintenance performed as a result of the prior owner's use does not qualify as routine maintenance and must be capitalized if the maintenance results in a betterment. Temp. Reg. § 1.263(a)-3T(g)(5), Ex.(4). However, although the maintenance ameliorates a known condition or defect at the time of acquisition of the machine, the proposed regulations would not treat the maintenance as a "betterment" requiring capitalization under Temp. Reg. § 1.263(a)-3T(h)(1)(i) because, depending on the facts and circumstances, regularly scheduled maintenance in accord with the manufacturer's recommendations, described as work of a minor nature that does not increase the capacity, etc., of the machine, does not ameliorate a material condition or defect. Temp. Reg. § 1.263(a)-3T(h)(4), Ex. (3).

The routine maintenance safe harbor also addresses maintenance performed with rotatable spare parts. Rotatable spare parts, such as engines in an aircraft, are parts that are removable from a unit of property, generally repaired or improved, and either reinstalled or stored for later use. Rotatable spare parts are treated as consumed in the taxpayer's trade or business in the year that the taxpayer disposes of the parts. Temp. Reg. § 1.162-3T(a)(3). The routine maintenance safe harbor of the temporary regulations includes maintenance of rotatable spare parts. Temp. Reg. § 1.263(a)-3T(g)(2). For example, an airline purchases an aircraft with four engines, the entire aircraft being a unit of property. Every four years the engines are removed from the aircraft for an engine shop visit in which the engines are disassembled, inspected, and repaired with the replacement of parts not meeting specifications; other engines are installed on the aircraft to keep it in service. After the shop visit the engines are reinstalled on another aircraft or stored for later use. The engines are rotatable spare parts. The recurring engine shop visit is treated as routine maintenance with respect to both the aircraft and the engines. Temp. Reg. § 1.263(a)-3T(g)(5), Ex.(1). The engine shop visit is treated as routine maintenance, even if undertaken after the end of the anticipated useful life of the aircraft. Temp. Reg. § 1.263(a)-3T(g)(5), Ex.(2).

3. EXPENSES IN CONNECTION WITH A PLAN OF REHABILITATION

In some situations the courts have held that an outlay, which if taken by itself would qualify for current deduction, must be capitalized if it is part of a more general plan involving the rehabilitation or improvement of property. Thus, in Griffin & Co. v. United States, 389 F.2d 802 (Ct.Cl.1968), the taxpayer incurred costs in relocating lighting fixtures in its offices in connection with changing the partition arrangement in the offices. The Court of Claims held that these expenditures were part of the taxpayer's program to improve its property and hence were required to be treated as capital expenditures. In Norwest Corp. v. Commissioner, 108 T.C. 265 (1997), the court rejected the taxpayer's argument that asbestos removal incident to general remodeling of a building should be viewed as a separate "repair" deductible under § 162; the asbestos removal was integral to a general rehabilitation of the building, which was a capital expense, because the asbestos would not have been removed if the remodeling had not occurred. See also Rev.Rul. 88–57, 1988–2 C.B. 36 (rehabilitation of railroad cars capitalized "even if standing alone rather than as part of a general scheme, would properly be classified as repairs"). These authorities are consistent with the majority opinions in *Mt. Morris*. Even if the expenditures in *Mt. Morris* would, taken by themselves, qualify as repairs, their relationship to the construction of the drive-in theater required capitalization. Under this view these expenditures are similar to the acquisition costs covered by *Woodward.*

However, Temp. Reg. § 1.263(a)-3T(f)(3)(i) rejects this judicial "plan of rehabilitation doctrine" and allows a current deduction for repairs and maintenance that do not directly benefit an improvement nor are incurred by reason of an improvement. Nevertheless, expenditures that otherwise would have been deductible as repairs but which contribute to a specific improvement that must be capitalized likewise must be capitalized. See Temp. Reg. § 1.263(a)-3T(h)(4), Ex. 9.

Pages 444-445:

Replace the carryover paragraph beginning at the bottom of page 444 with the following:

In Dominion Resources, Inc. v. United States, 219 F.3d 359 (4th Cir.2000), environmental remediation expenses were required to be capitalized rather than being deductible as repairs. To prepare the site of a retired power plant for use as an office building site or for sale, the taxpayer incurred remediation expenses to remove asbestos and other contaminants from the site. As a result, the appraised value of the property increased from approximately $1.5 million to approximately $9 million. Notwithstanding the holding of Rev. Rul. 94–38, 1994–1 C.B. 35, the taxpayer was required to capitalize the expenditures because the remediation altered the character of the property by enabling it to be put to "a wide range of new uses" as opposed to merely keeping the property in its ordinary efficient condition or restoring it to a condition that existed prior to deterioration or damage. *Dominion Resources* was followed in United Dairy Farmers, Inc. v. United States, 267 F.3d 510 (6th Cir.2001). The taxpayer incurred environmental remediation expenses to clean up pollution caused by prior owners who operated gas stations on the site of a convenience store. Even though the taxpayer was unaware of the pollution at the time of the purchase and thus "overpaid" for the property, it was required to capitalize the expenses because they "increased the value of the property." Rev. Rul. 94–38 did not apply. The Sixth Circuit concluded that "when a taxpayer improves property defects that were present when the taxpayer acquired the property, the remediation of those defects are capital in nature."

Temp. Reg. § 1.263(a)-3T(h)(4), Ex. (1) adopts the holding of *United Dairy Farmers*, indicating that the costs of amelioration of contamination existing prior to the taxpayer's purchase of property is a betterment to the land requiring that the costs be capitalized, even if the purchaser was unaware of the contamination at the time of purchase. On the other hand, Temp. Reg. § 1.263(a)-3T(j)(3), Ex. (4) indicates that cleanup of contamination from the taxpayer's manufacturing operation in preparation to sell the property to a developer who intends to develop the property for residential use is deductible. The example states that the clean-up of the taxpayer's manufacturing waste does not "adapt the land to a new or different use, regardless of the extent to which the land was cleaned." However, the example also indicates that expenditures incurred prior to sale to grade the land for residential development must be capitalized because those expenditures do adapt the land to a new or different use that is inconsistent with the taxpayer's intended ordinary use of the property at the time it was placed in service.

Page 445:

In the first full paragraph, fourth line from the bottom of the page, change the citation from Prop. Reg. § 1.263(a)-3(f)(3), Ex. (2) (2008) **to** Temp. Reg. § 1.263(a)-3T(h)(4), Ex. (2).

SECTION 4. BUSINESS INVESTIGATION, START-UP AND EXPANSION COSTS

Page 462:

Replace the third full paragraph with the following:

Treas. Reg. § 1.195-1(b) (2011) provides that a taxpayer is deemed to have elected to amortize start-up expenditures for the taxable year in which the active trade or business to which the expenditures relate begins. However, the taxpayer may forgo the deemed election "by affirmatively electing to capitalize its start-up expenditures on a timely filed Federal income tax return (including extensions) for the taxable year in which the active trade or business to which the expenditures relate begins." In either case, the decision whether or not to amortize start-up expenditures is irrevocable and applies to all start-up expenditures related to the active trade or business. A change in the characterization of an item as a start-up expenditure is a change of accounting method, which requires the consent of the IRS if the taxpayer treated the item consistently for two or more taxable years.

CHAPTER 14

COST RECOVERY MECHANISMS

SECTION 1. DEPRECIATION

A. ACCELERATED COST RECOVERY SYSTEM

Page 487:

Delete the first paragraph and insert:

Section 168(k)(1)(A), originally added by the 2002 Act, provides an additional stimulus to capital investment. For qualified property placed in service from January 1, 2012, until December 31, 2013, (from January 1, 2013, until December 31, 2014, for certain longer-lived and transportation property), taxpayers may claim first-year additional depreciation of 50 percent. Property placed in service after December 31, 2013 (December 31, 2014, for certain longer-lived and transportation property), will not be eligible for any additional first-year depreciation (absent legislative extension of § 168(k)) and therefore will be depreciated under the traditional rules. The adjusted basis of qualified property for purposes of calculating allowable depreciation is reduced by the amount of additional first-year depreciation provided by § 168(k) before applying the normal depreciation rules.

Page 488:

After the second full paragraph, insert:

Section 168(m), added in 2008, allows a special first-year depreciation deduction of 50 percent of the adjusted basis of "qualified reuse and recycling property." The balance of the adjusted basis is depreciated under the normal § 168 rules. Reuse and recycling property is machinery and equipment (including software necessary to operate such equipment) used exclusively to collect, distribute, or recycle qualified reuse and recyclable materials, other than equipment used to transport reuse and recyclable materials. Qualified reuse and recyclable materials include only scrap plastic, scrap glass, scrap textiles, scrap rubber, scrap packaging, recovered fiber, scrap ferrous and nonferrous metals, and certain electronic scrap (primarily central processing units and video display devices). Qualified property must have a useful life of at least five years, and the original use of the property must commence with the taxpayer. Ironically, previously used equipment does not qualify. The additional first-year depreciation for qualified reuse and recycling property cannot be claimed if the property is eligible for the general bonus depreciation rules in § 168(k).

B. Election to Expense Certain Depreciable Business Assets

Page 489:

After the last paragraph on the page, insert:

For tax years beginning in 2012, the maximum amount that a taxpayer may expense under § 179 is $125,000 of the cost of qualifying property placed in service during that year. The $125,000 amount is reduced by the amount by which the cost of qualifying property placed in service during the taxable year exceeds $500,000. For tax years beginning after 2012, the maximum amount and the phase-out threshold revert back to $25,000 and $200,000, respectively.

Replace footnote 9 with:

9. Expensing is applicable to off-the-shelf computer software that is placed in service in taxable years beginning after 2002 and before 2013. I.R.C. § 179(d)(1)(A)(ii).

Section 2. Statutory Amortization of Intangible Assets

Page 505:

At the end of the second full paragraph, add:

Recovery Group, Inc. v. Commissioner, 652 F.3d 122 (1st Cir. 2011), held that a $400,000 payment by a corporation to a retiring 23 percent shareholder/employee for a one-year covenant not to compete was amortizable over 15 years under § 197 because the covenant was part of an acquisition of an interest in a trade or business. The court rejected the taxpayer's argument that the term "§ 197 intangible" includes covenants not to compete executed in connection with stock purchases only if the stock being purchased comprises a substantial portion of the outstanding stock.

Section 3. Expensing and Amortization Provisions

Page 509:

At the end of the third full paragraph, add:

The deduction allowed by § 198 for environmental remediation expenses (which might otherwise be capital expenditures) expired on December 31, 2011, though it could be revived (perhaps retroactively back to January 1, 2012) through subsequent legislative action.

CHAPTER 15

TRANSACTIONAL LOSSES

SECTION 1. BUSINESS OR PROFIT SEEKING LOSSES

Page 530:

After the first full paragraph, insert:

A theft loss deduction is allowed with respect to criminally fraudulent Ponzi schemes. In response to the Bernie Madoff indictment, the IRS issued Rev. Rul. 2009-9, 2009-14 I.R.B. 735, which provides that defrauded investors may claim a theft loss deduction under § 165(c)(2). The amount of the deductible theft loss is equal to the excess of the investor's contributions over the sum of (i) the investor's withdrawals or other recoveries and (ii) the amount of any of the investor's claims as to which there is a reasonable prospect of future recovery. For this purpose, fictitious "earnings" on an investor's account that were previously reported as income by investor are treated as contributions by the investor. Thus, for example, if an investor originally contributed $100 of cash to a Madoff account, in Year 2 made an additional cash contribution of $20, in Year 3 withdrew $30 of cash from the account, and reported fictitious earnings of $60 in the years before becoming aware of the nature of Madoff's activities, the investor could claim a theft loss deduction of $150 in the year he became aware of the Ponzi scheme, assuming that he has no reasonable prospect of any future recovery. The IRS also ruled that, because the investors opened their investment accounts with the intent to enter into a transaction for profit, their theft losses were deductible under § 165(c)(2) (rather than §165(c)(3)) and, accordingly, the limitations in § 165(h) did not apply to these losses.

Simultaneously with the issuance of Rev. Rul. 2009-9, the IRS issued Rev. Proc. 2009-20, 2009-14 I.R.B. 749, which provides an elective safe harbor for investors victimized in criminally fraudulent Ponzi schemes. If they elect to take advantage of the safe harbor, investors who have pursued or intend to pursue a claim against any third-party (that is someone other than the perpetrator of the Ponzi scheme) must assume that they have a reasonable prospect of recovering (other than by way of insurance) 25 percent of their total potential theft loss; investors who do not intend to pursue a third-party claim must assume they have a reasonable prospect of recovering (other than by way of insurance) 5 percent of their total potential theft loss. If an investor's future recovery ultimately differs from these assumed amounts, the investor will realize an item of income or deduction in the year of recovery to reconcile the disparity.

SECTION 3. BAD DEBTS

Page 542:

After the third full paragraph, insert:

In Rendall v. Commissioner, 535 F.3d 1221 (10th Cir. 2008), the taxpayer lent $2 million to a publicly traded corporation. In 1997 the corporation declared bankruptcy and arranged the sale of most of its assets. However, the corporation retained rights to certain patents, and at the close of the year it was trading over-the-counter for $3 per share. The court affirmed the Tax Court's denial of a deduction for a worthless debt in 1997. The court held that the taxpayer had not established that the debt was worthless, which requires "identifiable events that form the basis of reasonable grounds for abandoning any hope of recovery." Quoting Roth Steel Tube Co. v. Commissioner, 620 F.2d 1176, 1182 (6th Cir. 1980), the court stated: "'Where a debtor company continues to operate as a going concern the courts have often concluded that its debts are not worthless for tax purposes despite the fact that it is technically insolvent.'"

CHAPTER 17

BUSINESS TAX CREDITS

[Editor's Note: As discussed below, many of the tax credits discussed in this chapter expired on December 31, 2011 and, at the time this supplement went to press, had not yet been extended. However, it is possible that many, if not all, of the tax credits that expired in 2011 will be retroactively extended through legislation enacted in late 2012 or early 2013.]

SECTION 2. GENERAL BUSINESS CREDIT

Page 579:

After the first full paragraph, insert:

The American Recovery and Reinvestment Act of 2009 added to the § 48 category of "energy properties" wind facilities eligible for the § 45 renewable electricity production credit placed in service in 2009 through 2012, and any other facility eligible for the § 45 renewable electricity production credit (with a few exceptions) placed in service in 2009 through 2013. If the energy credit is claimed for any such facility, the § 45 renewable electricity production credit cannot be claimed. The Act also added to the § 46 credit the new § 48C qualifying advanced energy credit, which provides a 30 percent credit for facilities that manufacture a wide array of alternative energy property.

Page 580:

At the end of the carryover paragraph, insert:

The work opportunity credit was extended until December 31, 2011.

Page 581:

After the second sentence of the second full paragraph, add:

The qualified research credit was extended until December 31, 2011.

Page 587:

Immediately before Section 3, add:

5. RETENTION OF NEWLY HIRED EMPLOYEES CREDIT

The 2010 Hiring Incentives to Restore Employment Act amended §§ 38(b) and 39 to provide a tax credit for retaining newly hired workers for at least 52 weeks. The amount of the credit is the lesser of (1) $1,000 or (2) 6.2 percent of the wages paid to a newly hired worker during the 52 week period following the commencement of employment. The credit is not available unless the employee's wages during the last 26 weeks of the period are at least 80 percent of the wages for the first 26 weeks of that period. The credit is allowed in the taxable year in which the 52 week period ends.

6. HEALTH INSURANCE CREDIT

The Patient Protection and Affordable Care Act of 2010 added § 45R, which adds to the § 38 general business credit a credit for health insurance expenses of certain small business employers, effective for taxable years beginning after 2010. This provision is intended to encourage small employers, who are not required to provide health insurance to their employees under the Act, to provide such insurance.

SECTION 3. OTHER BUSINESS CREDITS

Page 588:

Replace the last two sentences of the first full paragraph with the following:

For a business taxpayer, the credit generally may not exceed $50,000 with respect to all qualified property placed in service by the taxpayer during the taxable year at a particular location. The business credit is part of the general business credit. The credit is also available to a taxpayer installing a refueling facility on the grounds of his personal residence for personal use, but the maximum amount of the nonbusiness credit is $2,000. The credit generally is not available for property placed in service after 2011; for property relating to carbon, the credit is available for property placed in service before 2015.

At the end of the second full paragraph, insert:

The alcohol fuels credit was extended until December 31, 2011.

After the last sentence of the third full paragraph, add:

The biodiesel fuels credit was extended until December 31, 2011.

Page 589:

After the last sentence of the first full paragraph, add:

The renewable electricity production credit was extended until December 31, 2011.

Page 590:

Replace the last sentence of the third full paragraph with:

The credit was extended until December 31, 2011, such that it applied to homes purchased before that date.

After the last sentence of the fourth full paragraph, add:

The credit was extended to apply to appliances manufactured before 2012.

Replace the second sentence of the last paragraph with:

A CREB must be issued before January 1, 2010, by a qualified issuer—a governmental body, a cooperative energy company, or a "clean renewable energy bond lender."

Page 591:

After the last sentence of the first full paragraph, add:

The credit was extended until December 31, 2011.

Page 593:

At the end of the carryover paragraph, add:

The new markets credit has been extended through 2011, and the maximum nationwide aggregate annual credit limit is $3.5 billion for 2011.

Replace the last sentence of the last paragraph with:

The railroad track maintenance credit was extended until December 31, 2011.

After the last paragraph, insert:

Section 4. Additional Recently Enacted Credits

Since publication of the latest edition, Congress has continued to extend the effective dates of most existing business credits while simultaneously creating a host of new complicated credits. For example, as part of the Energy Improvement and Extension Act of 2008, Congress added a carbon sequestration credit (§45Q) to the general business credit and enacted credits for plug-in electric vehicles (§ 30D), new clean renewable energy bonds (§ 54C), and energy conservation bonds (§ 54D), while extending the effective dates of many of the existing energy-related credits. In the American Recovery and Reinvestment Act of 2009, Congress added the making work pay credit (§ 36A), the qualifying advanced energy product credit (§ 48C), the qualified school construction bond credit (§ 54F), the Build America bond credit (§ 54AA), and the recovery zone bond credit (§ 1400U). The Patient Protection and Affordable Care Act of 2010 added § 48D, which provides a credit equal to 50 percent of an eligible taxpayer's (generally speaking small businesses) "qualifying investment" with respect to any "qualifying therapeutic discovery project," aimed at developing a product, process, or therapy to diagnose, treat, or prevent diseases or afflictions.

PART IV

DUAL PURPOSE EXPENSES

CHAPTER 19

EXPENSES INVOLVING BOTH PERSONAL AND BUSINESS PURPOSES

SECTION 2. TRAVEL AND RELATED EXPENSES

Page 637:

After the Hantzis case, before the *Illustrative Material*, insert:

Wilbert v. Commissioner
United States Court of Appeals, Seventh Circuit, 2009.
553 F.3d 544.

■POSNER, CIRCUIT JUDGE, delivered the opinion of the Court.

The question presented by this appeal is whether an employee who uses "bumping" rights to avoid or postpone losing his job can deduct the living expenses that he incurs when he finds himself working far from home as a result of exercising those rights. The Tax Court ruled against the taxpayer,* * * assessing a deficiency of $ 4,380 in his income tax payments for 2003, and he appeals. This is one of a number of largely identical cases in the Tax Court,* * * all brought by mechanics formerly employed by Northwest Airlines, like Wilbert, and all resolved against the taxpayer. But this seems the first case to be appealed.

Hired by Northwest in 1996, Wilbert worked for the airline at the Minneapolis airport for some years. He lived with his wife in Hudson, Wisconsin, across the Mississippi River from Minneapolis. Hudson is a suburb of Minneapolis, roughly 25 miles from the airport.

Facing financial pressures and a decline in airline traffic in the wake of the terrorist attacks of September 11, 2001, Northwest laid off many employees, including, in April 2003, Wilbert. But Northwest's mechanics each had a right to bump a more junior mechanic employed by the airline, that is, to take his job. Wilbert was able to bump a mechanic who worked for the airline in Chicago, but he worked there for only a few days before being bumped by a more senior mechanic. A few days later he was able to bump a mechanic in Anchorage, Alaska, and he worked there for three weeks before being himself bumped. He was soon able to bump a mechanic who worked in New York, at LaGuardia Airport, but he worked there for only a week before he was bumped again. At this point, he had exhausted his bumping rights. But for reasons that the parties have not explained, three weeks later the airline hired him back, outside the bumping system, to fill an interim position (maximum nine months) in Anchorage. He occupied that position for several months before being laid off again, this time for good. At no point in his hegira did he have realistic prospects of resuming work for Northwest in Minneapolis. He now lives in a Chicago suburb and works for Federal Express at O'Hare Airport. He sells real estate on the side (self-employed), as he did when he lived in Minneapolis, but his income from his real estate business there was only $ 2,000 in 2003, the relevant tax year, and he did not actually receive the money (a commission) until the following year.

He did not sell or rent his home in Hudson, where his wife continued to live, while working intermittently in 2003. Because he was working too far from home to be able to live there, he incurred living expenses (amounting to almost $ 20,000) that he would not have incurred had he remained working in Minneapolis, and those are the expenses he deducted from the taxable income shown on his 2003 return.

The Internal Revenue Code allows the deduction, as part of "the ordinary and necessary expenses . . . incurred during the taxable year in carrying on any trade or business," of "traveling expenses . . . *while [the taxpayer is] away from home* in the pursuit of a trade or business." 26 U.S.C. § 162(a)(2) (emphasis added). There is an exception for "personal, living, or family expenses." § 262(a). The phrase we have italicized is critical. It is by an interpretation of that phrase that commuting expenses are disallowed because of "a natural reluctance . . . to lighten the tax burden of people who have the good fortune to interweave work with consumption. To allow a deduction for commuting would confer a windfall on people who live in the suburbs and commute to work in the cities." Moss v. Commissioner, 758 F.2d 211, 212 (7th Cir. 1985). The length of the commute is thus irrelevant. If Wilbert had had a permanent job in Anchorage but decided to retain his home in Minneapolis and return there on weekends and during the week live in a truck stop in Wasilla, Alaska, he could not have deducted from his taxable income the expense of traveling to and fro between Minnesota and Alaska or his room and board in Wasilla. (We ignore for the moment the possibility that Mrs. Wilbert had a job in Minneapolis, and if so its relevance.)

Similarly, he could not have deducted his traveling expenses if he had had no home separate from the places he traveled to--if he had been, in the language of the cases, an "itinerant" worker, for then he would never have been "away from home" on his travels. E.g., Fisher v. Commissioner, 230 F.2d 79 (7th Cir. 1956); Henderson v. Commissioner, 143 F.3d 497 (9th Cir. 1998); Deamer v. Commissioner, 752 F.2d 337 (8th Cir. 1985) (per curiam). He would have been like someone whose only residence is a recreational vehicle, or a truck driver who lives in the cab of his truck, or the taxpayer in the *Fisher* case — "an itinerant professional musician, [who] traveled from city to city performing, solo, in various hotel dining rooms and cocktail lounges. These engagements varied in duration from three to four weeks, or as long as seven or eight months. His wife and child traveled and lived with taxpayer wherever he was situated." 230 F.2d at 80.

With our hypothetical Wilbert the long-distance commuter, compare a lawyer whose home and office are both in Minneapolis but who has an international practice and as a result spends more time on the road than he does at home. Nevertheless he can deduct his traveling expenses. His work requires him to maintain a home within normal commuting distance of Minneapolis because that is where his office is, but his work also requires him to travel, and the expenses he incurs in traveling are necessary to his work and he cannot offset them by relocating his residence to the places to which he travels because he has to maintain a home near his office. And likewise if, as in Andrews v. Commissioner, 931 F.2d 132 (1st Cir. 1991), the taxpayer has to make such frequent trips to a particular site that it is more economical for him to rent or buy a second residence, at that site, than to live there in a hotel.

Wilbert's case falls in between our two hypothetical cases. Unlike the lawyer, he did not have to live near Minneapolis after the initial layoff because he had no work there (ignoring for the moment his real estate business). But unlike the imaginary Wilbert who has a permanent job in Alaska and so could readily relocate his home there, the real Wilbert had jobs of indefinite, unpredictable duration in Alaska (and Chicago, and New York). It would hardly have been realistic to expect him to pull up stakes and move to Anchorage and then to Chicago and then to New York and then back to Anchorage. Remember that his first stint after the initial layoff lasted only days, his second only weeks, and the third only one week. His situation was unlike that of the employee of a New York firm who, if he chooses to live in Scarsdale rather than on Fifth Avenue, is forbidden to deduct from his taxable income the commuting expense that he incurs by virtue of his choice; it is a personal choice--suburban over urban living--rather than anything necessitated by his job.

The Tax Court, with some judicial support, has tried to resolve cases such as this by asking whether the taxpayer's work away from home is "temporary" or "indefinite," and allowing the deduction of traveling expenses only if it is the former. E.g., Peurifoy v. Commissioner, 358 U.S. 59, * * * (1958) (per curiam); Kasun v. United States, 671 F.2d 1059 (7th Cir. 1982)* * *. The Internal Revenue Code does not explicitly adopt the distinction, but does provide (with an immaterial exception) that "the taxpayer shall not be treated as being temporarily away from home during any period of employment if such period exceeds 1 year." 26 U.S.C. § 162(a).

The problem with the Tax Court's distinction is that work can be, and usually is, both temporary and indefinite, as in our lawyer example. A lawsuit he is trying in London might settle on the second day, or last a month; his sojourn away from his office will therefore be both temporary *and* indefinite. Indeed *all* work is indefinite and much "permanent" work is really temporary. . An academic lawyer might accept a five-year appointment as an assistant professor with every expectation of obtaining tenure at the end of that period at that or another law school; yet one would not describe him as a "temporary" employee even if he left after six months and thus was not barred from claiming temporary status by the one-year rule. Our imaginary Wilbert who has a permanent job in Anchorage but is reluctant to move there from Minneapolis might argue (at least until he had worked a year, the statutory cutoff for "temporary" work) that no job is "permanent"--he might be fired, or he might harbor realistic hopes of getting a better job back in Minneapolis. That possibility would not permit him to deduct the expense of commuting from Minnesota to Alaska.

So "temporary versus indefinite" does not work well as a test of deductibility and neither does "personal choice versus reasonable response to the employment situation," tempting as the latter formula is because of its realism. If no reasonable person would relocate to his new place of work because of uncertainty about the duration of the new job, his choice to stay where he is, unlike a choice to commute from a suburb to the city in which one's office is located rather than live in the city, is not an optional personal choice like deciding to stay at a Four Seasons or a Ritz Carlton, but a choice forced by circumstances. Wilbert when first notified that he was being laid off could foresee a series of temporary jobs all across the country and not even limited, as we know, to the lower 48 states, and the costs of moving his home to the location of each temporary job would have been prohibitive. It would have meant moving four times in one year on a mechanic's salary to cities hundreds or (in the case of Anchorage versus Minneapolis, Chicago, or New York) thousands of miles apart.

The problem with a test that focuses on the reasonableness of the taxpayer's decision not to move is that it is bound to prove nebulous in application. For it just asks the taxpayer to give a good reason for not moving his home when he gets a job in a different place, and if he gave a good reason then his traveling expenses would be deductible as the product of a reasonable balancing of personal and business considerations. In the oft-cited case of Hantzis v. Commissioner, 638 F.2d 248 (1st Cir. 1981), the question was whether a law student who lived in Boston with her husband during the school year could deduct her traveling expenses when she took a summer job in New York. Given the temporary nature of the job, it made perfectly good sense for her to retain her home in Boston and just camp out, as it were, in New York. What persuaded the court to reject the deduction was that she had no *business* reason to retain the house in Boston. Id. at 255. Stated differently, she had no business reason to be living in two places at once, id. at 256, unlike the lawyer in our example. And so the expenses she incurred living in New York could not be thought "ordinary and *necessary* expenses . . . incurred . . . in carrying on any trade or business."

If this seems rather a mechanical reading of the statute, it has the support not only of the influential precedent of Hantzis but also of the even more influential precedent of Commissioner v. Flowers, 326 U.S. 465, 474,* * * (1946), where the Supreme Court said that "the exigencies of business rather than the personal conveniences and necessities of the traveler must be the motivating factors" in the decision to travel. The "business exigencies" rule, though harsh, is supported by compelling considerations of administerability. To apply a test of reasonableness the Internal Revenue Service would first have to decide whether the taxpayer should have moved to his new place of work. This might require answering such questions as whether the schools in the area of his new job were far worse than those his children currently attend, whether his elderly parents live near his existing home and require his attention, and whether his children have psychological problems that make it difficult for them to find new friends. Were it decided that it was reasonable for the taxpayer to stay put, it would then become necessary to determine whether the expenses he incurred in traveling to and from his various places of work for home visits had been reasonable--whether in other words such commutes, in point of frequency, were "ordinary and necessary" business expenses. The Internal Revenue Service would have to establish norms of reasonable home visits that presumably would vary with such things as distance and how many of the taxpayer's children were living at home and how old they were.

We are sympathetic to Wilbert's plight and recognize the artificiality of supposing that, as the government argues, he made merely a personal choice to "commute" from Minneapolis to Anchorage, and Chicago, and New York, as if Minneapolis were a suburb of those cities. But the statutory language, the precedents, and the considerations of administerability that we have emphasized persuade us to reject the test of reasonableness. The "temporary versus indefinite" test is no better, so we fall back on the rule of Flowers and Hantzis that unless the taxpayer has a business rather than a personal reason to be living in two places he cannot deduct his traveling expenses if he decides not to move.

Indeed, Wilbert's situation is really no different from the common case of the construction worker who works at different sites throughout the country, never certain how long each stint will last and reluctant therefore to relocate his home. The construction worker loses, as must Wilbert. E.g., Yeates v. Commissioner, 873 F.2d 1159 (8th Cir. 1989).

We might well have a different case if Wilbert had had a firm, justified expectation of being restored to his job at the Minneapolis airport within a short time of his initial layoff. Suppose the airline had said to him, "We must lay you off, but you will be able to bump a less senior employee in Anchorage for a few weeks, and we are confident that by then, given your seniority, you will be able to return to Minneapolis." His situation would then be comparable to that of a Minneapolis lawyer ordered by his senior partner to spend the next month trying a case in Anchorage. But that is not this case.

Wilbert has another string to his bow, however, arguing that he had two businesses, not one, the other being the sale of real estate, and that because that business was centered in Minneapolis he had a business reason to live near there. This would be a good argument if selling real estate were his main business. Andrews v. Commissioner, supra, 931 F.2d at 138; Ziporyn v. Commissioner, T.C. Memo 1997-151, * * *; Sherman v. Commissioner, 16 T.C. 332, 337 (1951)* * *. But obviously it is not, or at least was not in 2003, when his total income (and in an accrual rather than a cash sense) from selling real estate was only $ 2,000.

As explained in Andrews, "The guiding policy must be that the taxpayer is reasonably expected to locate his 'home,' for tax purposes, at his 'major post of duty' so as to minimize the amount of business travel away from home that is required; a decision to do otherwise is motivated not by business necessity but by personal considerations, and should not give rise to greater business travel deductions." 931 F.2d at 138. If Wilbert had had to travel back to Minneapolis from his new tax "homes" from time to time in order to attend to his real estate business, the travel expense (if the business was really the reason for the travel home), and conceivably even some of his living expenses at his home (his "secondary" home, in a tax sense, since his primary home for tax purposes would follow his work), might have been deductible, just as his expenses for the office equipment that he purchased in his real estate business were.* * * But he does not argue for such a deduction.

For completeness we note that if Wilbert's wife had a business in Minneapolis, this would make it all the more reasonable for Wilbert not to move away from Minneapolis. But it would not permit him to deduct his traveling expenses, because his decision to live with his wife (if only on occasional weekends) would (setting aside any considerations relating to his real estate sideline) be a personal rather than a business decision. Hantzis v. Commissioner, supra, 638 F.2d at 254 and n. 11 ("in this respect, Mr. and Mrs. Hantzis' situation is analogous to cases involving spouses with careers in different locations. Each must independently satisfy the requirement that deductions taken for travel expenses incurred in the pursuit of a trade or business arise while he or she is away from home"); Chwalow v. Commissioner, 470 F.2d 475, 477-78 (3d Cir. 1972)* * *.

Affirmed.

Page 640:

After the second full paragraph, insert:

In Lyseng v. Commissioner, T.C. Memo 2011-226, the Tax Court found that a travelling taxpayer's home was the personal residence that he shared with his father and his fiancé. The taxpayer was a contract laborer who performed maintenance work on nuclear plants and other utilities at temporary job sites that required travel away from his residence. The taxpayer's employment at any one job site lasted less than a year and was often for a period of a few months. Applying its tests from *Hantzis,* the Tax Court allowed the taxpayer's travel expense deductions holding that the taxpayer incurred duplicate expenses because the temporary nature of the work meant that the taxpayer had no principal place of business, the taxpayer had a personal and historic connections to the "home", and the taxpayer had a business justification for maintaining his home in the city where the union hall through which he obtained employment was located.

SECTION 3. BUSINESS MEALS AND ENTERTAINMENT

Page 656:

At the end of the fourth full paragraph, insert:

Section 274(h)(7) is strictly applied and will disallow deductions even where no entertainment or recreational activities are involved. Jones v. Commissioner, 131 T.C. 131 (2008), denied a deduction for a stock day trader who incurred approximately $6,000 of expenses to attend a 5-day one-on-one course consisting of 37 hours of instruction. The seminar was held in a small town in northwest Georgia, approximately 750 miles from the taxpayer's home in Florida. He stayed in a modest hotel and did not participate in any recreational activities. Citing Merriam-Webster's Collegiate Dictionary (9th ed. 1985), which defines a seminar as a "meeting for giving and discussing information," the court concluded that the course was a seminar, or a similar meeting within the scope of § 274(h)(7).

CHAPTER 19 EXPENSES INVOLVING BOTH PERSONAL AND BUSINESS PURPOSES

SECTION 4. STATUTORY LIMITATIONS ON DEDUCTIONS FOR CERTAIN PROPERTY

Page 659:

At the end of the second full paragraph, add:

In 2010, Congress removed cellular telephones from the definition of "listed property."

Page 661:

At the end of the third full paragraph, add:

In 2010, Congress removed cellular telephones from the definition of "listed property."

PART V

DEDUCTIONS AND CREDITS FOR PERSONAL LIVING EXPENSES

CHAPTER 21

ITEMIZED PERSONAL DEDUCTIONS

SECTION 2. MEDICAL EXPENSES

Page 701

At the end of the last paragraph, add:

The "medical care" standard under § 213(d) requires a causal relationship between an underlying medical condition or defect and the taxpayer's expenses, and the expenses must be incurred for the purpose of affecting a structure or function of the taxpayer's body. Magdalin v. Commissioner, T.C. Memo. 2008-293, denied a medical expense deduction for the costs incurred in fathering children through unrelated gestational carriers via in vitro fertilization of an anonymous donor's eggs using the taxpayer's sperm. There was not a causal relationship between an underlying medical condition or defect because taxpayer's sperm count and

CHAPTER 21 ITEMIZED PERSONAL DEDUCTIONS   47

motility were found to be within normal limits, and the expenses at issue were not incurred to affect a structure or function of the taxpayer's body.

Page 703:

After the carryover paragraph, insert:

In O'Donnabhain v. Commissioner, 134 T.C. 34 (2010), the Tax Court held that the costs of hormone therapy and male-to-female sex reassignment surgery to treat gender identity disorder, which is a condition recognized in medical reference texts, are deductible as medical expenses, reasoning that the procedure is not "cosmetic surgery" as defined by the statute. However, the cost of breast augmentation was not deductible; it was cosmetic surgery because the only purpose was to alter taxpayer's appearance.

Page 710:

At the end of the section, insert:

8. IMPACT OF PATIENT PROTECTION AND AFFORDABLE CARE ACT OF 2010

The far-reaching Patient Protection and Affordable Care Act of 2010, if and when it becomes fully operative, will affect the tax treatment of medical expenses. The Act amends § 213 to increase the 7.5 percent adjusted gross income limitation for deducting unreimbursed medical expenses to 10 percent for taxable years beginning after December 31, 2012. However, the increased threshold does not apply for years 2013 through 2016 if either the taxpayer or the taxpayer's spouse turns 65 before the end of the year. The 10 percent adjusted gross income increased threshold for deducting medical expenses under the alternative minimum tax is unaffected.

The primary purpose of the Act is to reduce the number of uninsured individuals. Because more health care expenses presumably will be covered by insurance, the importance of § 213, which applies only to unreimbursed expenses, should be reduced. To encourage people to purchase health insurance, the Act imposes a "penalty" (tax) through the tax Code on persons who fail to acquire "minimum essential health insurance coverage." The penalty, which is imposed under new § 5000A, phases-in beginning in January 2014, and it becomes fully effective in 2016. The penalty applies month-by-month, but there is a once per year exception for a coverage gap of less than three consecutive months. The monthly penalty is 1/12 of an annualized penalty amount. Beginning in 2016, the annualized penalty is the greater of: (1) 2.5 percent of the amount by which the taxpayer's household income for the taxable year exceeds the threshold amount of income requiring an income tax return to be filed for that year, or (2) $695 per uninsured adult in the household (indexed for inflation after 2016). The penalty for an uninsured individual under age 18 is one-half of the penalty for an adult. During the phase-in period (2014 through 2015), the adult penalty is a fixed $95 for 2014 and $325 for 2015. There are limits on the aggregate household penalty that is imposed. The penalty is due upon notice and demand, and it is subject to normal assessment procedures. However, the penalty cannot be collected by lien and levy. There are no criminal or civil penalties for failure to pay, and interest does not accrue on late payments.

Whether this so-called "individual mandate" is a constitutionally permissible exercise of Congress's taxing power or power to regulate interstate commerce was the subject of much debate. Immediately after the law was enacted, a large number of plaintiffs rushed to file lawsuits claiming that the mandate was impermissible. In a 5-4 decision the Supreme Court upheld the individual mandate as a permissible exercise of the Congress's taxing power. National Federation of Independent Business v. Sebelius, 567 U.S. ___ (6/28/12).

Another purpose of the Patient Protection and Affordable Care Act is to control health care costs. Economists have criticized the tax law's historic unlimited exclusion for employer-provided health insurance. This treatment created an incentive for employers to provide more generous health insurance plans (so-called "Cadillac plans") than they would have provided if health insurance benefits were taxable. Cadillac plans included lower co-pays, lower deductibles, and more flexibility, all of which encourage overuse of medical services that leads to increased prices for these services. To mitigate this problem, economists suggested that the exclusion for employer-provided health insurance be capped at a reasonable amount. Employees could still obtain "excess" insurance, but the excess amount now would be taxed just like cash. By removing the distortion in favor of excess health insurance over cash, economists expected that employers would offer more modest health insurance plans and pass the savings on to employees in the form of higher cash salaries. While this all made sense in theory, it became clear that it was politically unfeasible to tax employees on Cadillac plans. Instead, Congress enacted new § 4890I, which imposes an excise tax on insurers who provide Cadillac insurance. The effect should be the same as a tax on the employee because insurers will increase the prices of Cadillac plans to reflect the additional cost of issuing them. The excise tax is equal to 40 percent (which, notably, is higher than the current maximum federal marginal tax rate) of the excessive component of the employee's insurance.

To help pay for the subsidies that will be provided for lower income individuals to purchase health insurance, Congress added § 5000B, which imposes a 10 percent excise tax on the amount paid for indoor tanning services. The tax is collected by the service provider and remitted to the IRS quarterly. The tax became effective on July 1, 2010.

SECTION 3. CHARITABLE CONTRIBUTIONS

Page 722:

At the end of the carryover paragraph, add:

The Tax Court's decision in *Sklar* was affirmed on appeal. Sklar v. Commissioner, 549 F.3d 1252 (9th Cir. 2008). The Ninth Circuit followed its earlier decision involving different taxable years, Sklar v. Commissioner, 282 F.3d 610 (9th Cir. 2002)) and denied the taxpayers' claimed deductions of a portion of tuition and fees paid to Orthodox Jewish Day schools for the education of their children. The court held under *Hernandez*, text, page 711, tuition paid for religious education is a payment for services that is not deductible as a charitable contribution. The taxpayer had not established that the payments included an amount in excess of the value of the education benefit provided by the schools. The court reasoned that an attempt to distinguish payments for religious benefits from secular services would involve the court in impermissible entanglements between church and state.

Page 723:

In the first full paragraph, before the last sentence, add:

See also Durden v. Commissioner, T.C. Memo. 2012-140, denying a charitable contribution deduction of over $250, where the letter from the donee church failed to indicate that no goods or services were provided to the taxpayer.

Page 728:

After the first full paragraph, insert:

In Jones v. Commissioner, 560 F.3d 1196 (10th Cir. 2009), one of Timothy McVeigh's lawyers in the criminal trial stemming from the 2000 Oklahoma City Federal Building bombing donated to the University of Texas copies of documents received by him from the government in the course of his representation of McVeigh and claimed a charitable contribution deduction for the appraised value. The Tenth Circuit denied the deduction because the discovery material was not a capital asset and the taxpayer had a zero basis. The discovery material for which Jones claimed a charitable contribution deduction, which was first compiled by the government to assist in its investigation and copies of which were made, organized, and categorized by the government and delivered to the taxpayer for the benefit of Jones and his client, was not a capital asset because it constituted letters, memoranda, or similar property "prepared or produced" for the taxpayer within the meaning of § 1221(a)(3)(B).

Page 730:

After the third full paragraph, insert the following paragraph:

In Rolfs v. Commissioner, 668 F.3d 888 (7th Cir. 2012), the Seventh Circuit considered whether a charitable deduction was allowed when the taxpayers donated their house to the local fire department so that it could be burned down in a firefighter training exercise. The taxpayers, who desired the demolition in order to build another house on the property, claimed a $76,000 charitable deduction, based on before and after appraisals of the property. The court rejected that valuation approach in this context, instead concluding that, "[w]hen property is donated to a charity on the condition that it must be destroyed, that condition must be taken into account when valuing the gift." As a result, the value of the gift by the taxpayers did not exceed the fair market value of the benefit (i.e., the demolition of the house) that they received in return and, accordingly, no charitable deduction was allowed.

Page 731:

After the third full paragraph, insert:

In Mohamed v. Commissioner, T.C. Memo. 2012-152, the Tax Court applied a strict adherence to the substantiation requirements. The taxpayer claimed over $3,000,000 of charitable contribution deductions on the transfer of real property to a charitable remainder trust for which the taxpayer was the trustee. The taxpayer was a real estate broker and certified real estate appraiser. The taxpayer prepared his own tax returns and, although the taxpayer attached statements to his return for the year describing the donated property, the taxpayer did not attach a qualified appraisal as required by Treas. Reg. § 1.170A-13(c). The Tax Court granted summary judgment to the IRS upholding the validity of the substantiation regulations and finding that the taxpayer failed to satisfy the "substantial compliance doctrine" which allows minor deviations from the substantiation requirements but which cannot substitute for the absence of the qualified appraisal. In addition, a subsequent independent appraisal prepared for the taxpayer in the course of the audit that showed valuations slightly higher than claimed by the taxpayer did not substitute for the qualified appraisal required to be filed with the taxpayer's return claiming the deductions.

Page 734:

At the end of the first full paragraph, add:

Kaufman v. Commissioner, 134 T.C. 182 (2010), held that no charitable contribution deduction is allowable for the conveyance of an otherwise qualifying conveyance of a facade conservation easement if the property is subject to a

CHAPTER 21   ITEMIZED PERSONAL DEDUCTIONS   51

mortgage and the mortgagee has a prior claim to condemnation and insurance proceeds. Because the mortgage has priority over the easement, the easement is not protected in perpetuity, which is required by § 170(h)(5)(A).

SECTION 4. STATE AND LOCAL TAXES

Page 740:

After the second sentence of the second full paragraph, insert:

The election to deduct state sales taxes was extended until 2011. As of the date of the publication of this supplement, the state sales tax deduction had not yet been extended further, though it is possible that Congress will retroactively reinstate the deduction back to January 1, 2012.

SECTION 5. QUALIFIED HOME MORTGAGE INTEREST

Page 744:

After the first full paragraph, insert the following paragraph:

In Sophy v. Commissioner, 138 T.C. No. 8 (2012), two unmarried individuals co-owned two residences. At issue was how the $1,000,000 limitation on acquisition indebtedness and the $100,000 limitation on home equity indebtedness were to be applied in such a situation. The taxpayers argued that the aggregate $1.1 million limitation was to be applied on a per-taxpayer basis with respect to residence co-owners who are not married to each other. Based on a careful parsing of the language in § 163(h)(3), the Tax Court disagreed, concluding that Congress intended the limitation to be applied on a per-residence basis. Accordingly, the taxpayers' aggregate deductions for mortgage interest was limited to the interest that they paid on $1.1 million of the loans that were secured by the two residences.

Page 746:

At the end of the second full paragraph, add:

The deduction for mortgage insurance premiums was extended by Congress until December 31, 2011.

Page 747:

At the end of the carryover paragraph from page 746, insert:

However, in Rev. Rul. 2010-25, 2010-44 I.R.B. 571, the IRS backed off of its victory in *Pau*, concluding that "home equity indebtedness" (within the meaning of § 163(h)(3)(C)(i)) does include acquisition indebtedness exceeding $1,000,000.

CHAPTER 22

STANDARD DEDUCTION, PERSONAL AND DEPENDENCY EXEMPTIONS, AND PERSONAL CREDITS

SECTION 1. PERSONAL EXEMPTIONS AND THE STANDARD DEDUCTION

B. PERSONAL EXEMPTIONS

Page 768:

At the end of the last paragraph on the page, add:

The definition of a qualifying child has been amended to require that a qualifying child (1) must not have filed a joint return with a spouse (other than to claim a refund) and (2) must be younger than the taxpayer.

Page 769:

After the second full paragraph, insert:

Under Treas. Reg. § 1.152-4, for purposes of § 152(e) the custodial parent is the parent with whom the child spends the greatest number of nights during the taxable year. A child who is temporarily away is treated as spending the night with the parent with whom the child would have resided. If another person is entitled to custody for a night, the child is treated as spending the night with neither parent. On a school day, the child is treated as residing at the primary residence registered with the school. The regulations also provide that the required written declaration to surrender the exemption to the noncustodial parent must contain an *unconditional* statement that the custodial parent will not claim the exemption for the specified year or years; a declaration that conditions the custodial parent's release of the right to claim to the exemption on the noncustodial parent meeting a support obligation is not valid. A copy of the written declaration must be attached to the tax return for each year the noncustodial parent claims the exemption. The custodial parent may revoke a revocation by providing written notice to the non-custodial parent specifying the years of the revocation. Once a child reaches the age of majority under state law, generally age 18, the child is not in the custody of either parent (or anyone else) for purposes of § 152. Boltinghouse v. Commissioner, T.C. Memo. 2007-324.

SECTION 2. PERSONAL CREDITS

A. CREDITS FOR BASIC LIVING EXPENSES

(1) EARNED INCOME CREDIT

Page 773:

Replace the first full paragraph with the following:

The American Recovery and Reinvestment Tax Act of 2009 added § 32(b)(3) to increase the credit for taxpayers with three or more children to 45 percent of earned income up to $12,570 for taxable years 2009 and 2010. The Act also amended § 32(b)(2)(B) for 2009 and 2010 to increase the phase-out threshold for joint returns to $5,000 more than the phase-out threshold for single returns (subject to an inflation adjustment after 2009). These changes were subsequently extended through 2012.

The inflation-adjusted credit bases and phase-out thresholds for 2012 are as follows.

Number of Qualifying Children

Item	One	Two	Three or More	None
Earned Income Amount	$9,320	$13,090	$13,090	$6,210
Maximum Amount of Credit	$3,169	$5,236	$5,891	$475
Threshold Phase-out Amount (Single, Surviving Spouse, or Head of Household)	$17,090	$17,090	$17,090	$7,770
Completed Phase-out Amount (Single, Surviving Spouse, or Head of Household)	$36,920	$41,952	$45,060	$13,980
Threshold Phase-out Amount (Married Filing Jointly)	$22,300	$22,300	$22,300	$12,980
Completed Phase-out Amount (Married Filing Jointly)	$42,130	$47,162	$50,270	$19,190

Rev. Proc. 2011-52, 2011-2 C.B. 701, §2.06(1).

Even though the threshold for the phase-out is higher for married couples filing a joint return than it is for heads of households, the phase-out rules result in a significant "tax penalty" to marriage by low income individuals eligible for the earned income tax credit.

(2) THE CHILD CREDIT

Page 775:

After the first sentence of the second paragraph, insert:

Section 24(a) requires that the taxpayer be eligible to claim the child as a dependent under § 151 as a prerequisite to claiming the child credit.

After the third sentence of the second paragraph, insert:

The $1,000 child tax credit has been extended through 2012.

After the last paragraph on the page, add:

The American Recovery and Reinvestment Tax Act of 2009 amended § 24(d) to make the child tax credit refundable for 2009 and 2010 to the extent of 15 percent of the taxpayer's earned income in excess $3,000. That rule was subsequently extended through 2012.

B. TAX CREDITS FOR PERSONAL COSTS

Page 780:

In the second full paragraph, change the first sentence to:

Section 23 provides a refundable credit of up to $13,170 (adjusted for inflation after 2010) per child for qualified adoption expenses paid or incurred by individual taxpayers.

In the third full paragraph, replace the fourth sentence with the following:

Although the credit was originally nonrefundable, the Patient Protection and Affordable Care Act of 2010 made the credit refundable for 2010 and subsequent taxable years. However, the refundability feature is scheduled to expire on December 31, 2012.

Page 781:

Replace the last sentence of the second paragraph with the following:

The credit is available only for property placed in service before 2017.

CHAPTER 23

TAX EXPENDITURES FOR EDUCATION

Page 785:

After the first full paragraph, insert:

[Ed: The American Recovery and Reinvestment Tax Act of 2009 temporarily increased the Hope Scholarship Credit to the sum of (1) 100 percent of the first $2,000 of tuition, fees, and course materials paid during the taxable year, and (2) 25 percent of the next $2,000. The maximum credit is $2,500. I.R.C. § 25A(i). The temporarily increased credit has been named the "American Opportunity Tax Credit." The American Opportunity Tax Credit is allowed with respect to any of the first four years of post-secondary education (in lieu of the first two years rule under the HOPE credit). Thus, the credit can be claimed with respect to a student with respect to whom the credit already had been claimed for two years. Further, the cost of "course materials," in addition to tuition and fees, is now eligible for the credit. The revised credit can be claimed against the alternative minimum tax. Forty percent of the allowable credit is refundable, unless the taxpayer is a child subject to the § 1(g) "kiddie tax." (For § 1(g), see text, page 1312.) The American Opportunity Tax Credit is phased out for taxpayers with adjusted gross incomes in excess of $80,000 ($160,000 for married couples filing jointly), under the same formula as the Hope Scholarship Credit. The American Opportunity Tax Credit is scheduled to expire on December 31, 2012, at which time the Hope Scholarship Credit would return.]

Page 786:

At the end of the fifth full paragraph, delete the bracketed sentence and insert:

[Ed. The § 222 deduction expired on December 31, 2011; however, it is possible that Congress will retroactively reinstate the deduction, though it had not done so at the time this supplement went to press.]

PART VI

CHARACTERIZATION OF GAINS AND LOSSES

CHAPTER 24

CAPITAL GAINS AND LOSSES

SECTION 1. SPECIAL TREATMENT OF CAPITAL GAINS AND LOSSES

[Editor's Note: The capital gains tax rates described in this section were originally scheduled to expire on December 31, 2010, but they have since been extended until December 31, 2012. If they are not further extended, the capital gains rates will revert back to the pre-2003 capital gains tax rates; thus, most long-term capital gains would be taxed at 20 percent, rather than the current 15 percent rate.]

Page 804:

After the carryover paragraph, insert:

Beginning in 2013, investment income will be subject to an additional 3.8 percent income tax surtax when it is earned by certain higher-income individuals. While the tax, imposed by new § 1411, technically is an employment tax provision, it operates as income tax surtax. The surtax applies to the lesser of (1) net investment income or (2) the excess of adjusted gross income over a threshold amount. The threshold amount is $250,000 for spouses filing a joint return and

$200,000 for single taxpayers. The surtax was enacted to help fund the subsidies provided to lower-income individuals to purchase health insurance. Investment income includes capital gains, so the effective federal tax rate for these gains will be 3.8 percentage points higher when the surtax applies. Thus, for example, the effective federal tax rate on long-term capital gains recognized by high-income individuals would be increased from 15 percent to 18.8 percent (or from 20 percent to 23.8 percent if the reduction from 20 percent to 15 percent enacted in 2003 is allowed to expire, as it is scheduled to do, after 2012).

Page 809:

Replace the second sentence of footnote 2 with the following:

This provision is scheduled to expire on December 31, 2012.

Page 817:

Replace the last sentence of the carryover paragraph with the following:

The current capital gains rates originally were scheduled to sunset after December 31, 2010, but subsequent legislation extended them through December 31, 2012. Absent further legislation, the pre-2003 version of § 1(h), with its slightly higher rates will again be in force starting in 2013.

Page 822:

After the fourth full paragraph, insert:

The additional preference for qualified small business stock was temporarily enhanced. For qualified small business stock acquired from February 18, 2009 through September 27, 2010, 75 percent (rather than 50 percent) of the gain recognized from the disposition of such stock was eligible for exclusion. For qualified small business stock acquired from September 28, 2010, through December 31, 2011, 100 percent of the gain was eligible for exclusion. The traditional 50 percent exclusion applies for qualified small business stock acquired after December 31, 2011.

Section 2. Definition of Capital Asset

B. Judicial Limitations on Capital Asset Classification

Page 873:

After the last paragraph, insert:

2.1.1 Life Insurance Contracts

The substitute for ordinary income principle is not rigorously applied to gains from the sale of life insurance policies. Rev. Rul. 2009-13, 2009-21 I.R.B. 1029, held that if a life insurance contract with a cash surrender value is sold by the insured to an unrelated person who would not suffer loss if the beneficiary died, only the portion of the gain realized on the sale that reflects the inside build-up of the cash surrender value immediately prior to the sale is ordinary income, and any excess amount is capital gain, even though if the entire policy were surrendered to the insurer for cash, all of the gain would be ordinary income. (The amount of gain realized on a sale is the amount received on the sale minus the adjusted basis in contract, which is the amount of premiums paid minus an amount to properly reflect "cost of insurance.") If a term life insurance contract with no cash surrender value is sold, the entire amount recognized is long-term capital gain; because the cost of insurance each month is presumed to be equal to the premiums paid, there is no inside build-up under the contract. Rev. Rul. 2009-14, 2009-21 I.R.B. 1031, held that all of the gain recognized on sale of a life insurance policy by a taxpayer who had purchased the policy as an investment from the insured, to whom the policy had originally been issued, and who had no insurable interest is capital gain, notwithstanding that the full amount of the proceeds minus the basis in the contract is ordinary income if the purchaser holds the contract until the insured's death and collects the death benefit.

2.1.2 State Tax Credits

In CCA 201147024, the IRS concluded that nonrefundable, transferable state tax credits were capital assets if the tax credits do not fall within the statutory exclusions in §1221(a). The CCA was issued after the taxpayer had prevailed on the issue in Tempel v. Commissioner, 136 T.C. 341 (2011) and McNeil v. Commisioner, T.C. Memo. 2011-109. In these cases, the Tax Court rejected the government's argument that the substitute for ordinary income doctrine applied to treat the tax credit as an ordinary asset.

CHAPTER 25

SALES OF ASSETS HELD FOR USE IN A TRADE OR BUSINESS

SECTION 2. SALE OF AN ENTIRE BUSINESS

Page 916:

After the second full paragraph, insert:

A question sometimes arises regarding the identity of the owner and seller of business goodwill when the assets of a business owned by a closely held corporation are sold. In most cases, the business goodwill clearly is owned by the corporation and not by the shareholders. However, in a few cases shareholders who were the primary entrepreneurs and key employees argued that some or all of the business goodwill was owned by them individually. In Martin Ice Cream Co. v. Commissioner, 110 T.C. 189 (1998), Häagen-Dazs repurchased the rights to distribute Häagen-Dazs ice cream in the United States from the business that had been distributing Häagen-Dazs under an oral agreement between Häagen-Dazs and the majority shareholder. The IRS treated the amounts received in consideration of the distributorship rights as an amount realized by the corporation, but the corporation and its majority shareholder argued that the amounts were received directly by the shareholder. The Tax Court agreed with the taxpayers, holding that the shareholder, rather than the corporation, owned the distribution rights and sold them back to Häagen-Dazs, reasoning that the rights were based on the shareholder's personal relationships with supermarket chains and the shareholder's personal oral agreement with the founder of Häagen-Dazs, which never became a corporate asset. A similar result was reached in Norwalk v. Commissioner, T.C. Memo 1998-279, which involved a CPA professional services corporation that dissolved and distributed its assets to its two CPA shareholders, who in turn contributed the assets to a partnership that they joined in that year. The IRS asserted that in addition to the tangible assets expressly distributed, the corporation distributed various customer based intangible assets, including goodwill, which resulted in a gain to the corporation under § 336, which requires a distributing corporation to recognize gain when appreciated assets are distributed to shareholders in the same manner as if the corporation had sold the assets for fair market value. The Tax Court agreed with the taxpayer's contention that the corporation's earnings were entirely attributable to the CPA-shareholders — any clients would have followed the individual CPAs — and that the corporation, therefore, owned no goodwill that could be separately sold. The court reasoned that on the facts clients sought the personal ability, personality, and reputation of the individual CPAs, and these assets did not belong to the corporation; the corporation's name and its business location did not contribute to goodwill.

Martin Ice Cream and *Norwalk* were distinguished in Solomon v. Commissioner, T.C. Memo. 2008-102. Solomon Colors, Inc. sold one of its businesses to another corporation. In connection with the sale, the Solomons (father and son), who were majority shareholders and key employees, entered into covenants not to compete. Provisions in the contracts described payments received by the taxpayers as consideration for their execution of the covenants not to compete, but other documents allocating the purchase price and payments among assets described those payments as consideration for the shareholder's ownership interest in the customer list for the business that was sold. The court rejected the taxpayers' argument that, as in *Martin Ice Cream Co.*, the payments were consideration for the sale of goodwill owned by the shareholders. The *Solomon* court found that the value of the Solomon Colors' business was not attributable to the quality of service and customer relationships developed by the shareholders, which distinguished the facts from *Martin Ice Cream Co.* Because the Solomon Colors' business involved processing, manufacturing, and sale of a product, rather than the provision of services, the corporation's success did not depend entirely on the personal goodwill of its shareholder/employees. Furthermore, the fact that the purchaser did not require the shareholders to enter into employment or consulting agreements made it unlikely that it was purchasing their personal goodwill. Accordingly, the payments were entirely consideration for the shareholders' covenants not to compete and thus were ordinary income, not capital gain.

Muskat v. United States, 554 F.3d 183 (1st Cir. 2009), reached a similar result. The taxpayer was the chief executive officer and owner of 37 percent of the outstanding stock of a corporation, all of the stock of which was acquired by another corporation. In connection with the acquisition, the taxpayer entered into an employment agreement and a noncompetition agreement. The noncompetition agreement provided for payments over thirteen years, and the payments would survive the taxpayer's death. The taxpayer claimed that the payments under the noncompetition agreement were in fact payments for personal goodwill, and thus should have been taxed as capital gains rather than ordinary income. The court held that when the parties to a transaction have executed a written instrument allocating the purchase price to particular items, and one party thereafter seeks to alter the written allocation for tax purposes, that party "must adduce 'strong proof' that, at the time of execution of the instrument, the contracting parties actually intended the payments to compensate for something different. ... [The party] seeking to alter a written allocation must demonstrate an actual meeting of the minds with respect to some other allocation." Strong proof would require evidence having "persuasive power closely resembling the 'clear and convincing' evidence required to reform a written contract on the ground of mutual mistake."

The record did not contain any evidence of discussions of the taxpayer's personal goodwill during the negotiations, and none of the transaction documents (including drafts) mentioned his personal goodwill. Furthermore, the purchaser's president testified that "he could not imagine that any goodwill other than [the corporation's] was material to the transaction." The court held for the government because the taxpayer "had failed to adduce strong proof that the contracting parties intended the challenged payment to be compensation for personal goodwill."

PART VII

DEFERRED RECOGNITION OF GAIN FROM PROPERTY

CHAPTER 26

LIKE-KIND EXCHANGES

SECTION 2. MULTIPARTY AND DEFERRED EXCHANGES

Page 944:

At the end of the last paragraph, add:

The Ninth Circuit affirmed the Tax Court's decision in Teruya Bros., Ltd., text, page 944, stating, "it appears that these transactions took their peculiar structure for no purpose except to avoid § 1031(f).... Teruya could have achieved the same property dispositions through far simpler means." 580 F.3d 1038 (9th Cir. 2009). As in *Teruya Bros., Ltd*, in Ocmulgee Fields, Inc. v. Commissioner, 132 T.C. 105 (2009), aff'd, 613 F.3d 1360 (11th Cir. 2010), the Tax Court applied § 1031(f) to deny § 1031 treatment to a deferred three-corner exchange involving related parties. In the *Ocmulgee Fields* transaction, the taxpayer transferred appreciated real property (Wesleyan Station) to a qualified intermediary, an unrelated third party purchased the Wesleyan Station property from the qualified intermediary for cash, a partnership related to the taxpayer sold like-kind property (Barnes & Noble Corner) to the qualified intermediary for cash, and the qualified intermediary transferred the like-kind Barnes & Noble Corner property to the taxpayer. Apart from § 1031(f)(4), the exchange with the qualified intermediary would have qualified for § 1031 nonrecognition. The taxpayer argued that the transaction was not structured to attempt to avoid § 1031(f), because the reason it acquired the replacement property from the related partnership was that it was unable to locate a suitable replacement property within the time limits imposed on deferred like-kind exchanges under § 1031(a)(3) and Treas. Reg. § 1.1031(k)-1(b). That argument was factually tenuous, however, because the taxpayer entered into the agreement to acquire the replacement property only five days after the relinquished property was sold and closed the purchase before the 45-day identification period had even lapsed. Thus, the court held that tax-free like-kind exchange treatment was not available because the taxpayer had "structured" the transaction "to avoid the purposes" of the rule of § 1031(f). The court found that the "basis shift," which resulted from the transaction, established the requisite principal purpose of tax avoidance. The basis shift effected an approximately $1.8 million reduction in taxable gain, because if the related partnership had acquired Wesleyan Station from the taxpayer in a like-kind exchange for Barnes & Noble Corner, the related partnership's substituted basis in Wesleyan Station, which in the taxpayer's hands was only approximately $716,000, would have been approximately $2,555,000 (equal to the related person's basis in Barnes & Noble Corner). Furthermore, if § 1031 had applied, the gain on the sale of Wesleyan Station would have been taxed at only 15 percent, the applicable rate for capital gains taxed to the partners of the related partnership, instead of the 34 percent rate that would have applied had the taxpayer corporation sold the property. The taxpayer argued that unlike the taxpayer in *Teruya Bros.*, it did not have a prearranged plan to use property from a related person to complete a like-kind exchange, but the court concluded that the presence of the prearranged plan in *Teruya Bros.* was not a critical element of the holding in that case.

PART VIII

TIMING OF INCOME AND DEDUCTIONS

CHAPTER 28

TAX ACCOUNTING METHODS

SECTION 2. THE CASH METHOD

A. INCOME ITEMS

Page 980:

Replace the third from last sentence of the last paragraph with the following:

Generally speaking, if adequate interest is charged, the adjusted issue price of the debt obligation will be equal to its stated principal amount.

SECTION 3. THE ACCRUAL METHOD

A. INCOME ITEMS

Page 1003:

After the first full paragraph, insert:

In Trinity Industries, Inc. v. Commissioner, 132 T.C. 6 (2009), the taxpayer built barges for customers and part of the payment of the purchase price was contractually deferred until 18 months after delivery of each barge. Before having completed payment for some barges, the purchasers claimed there were defects in other previously purchased barges and asserted a common law right to offset their claimed damages against the deferred payments. When the customer withheld payment, the taxpayer included only the payments actually received and excluded the deferred payments, which ordinarily would have been accrued as income. The Tax Court held that the full contract price was includable in the year the barges were delivered, and the amount that should have been accrued as income could not be reduced by amounts withheld by the purchasers under their asserted right to offset claimed damages. The customer's offset affected only the timing of the taxpayer's receipt of the sales proceeds, not its right to receive the proceeds, because the taxpayer subsequently "received" the withheld amounts when, pursuant a settlement agreement, the withheld amounts were applied in compromise of the purchaser's claims for damages.

CHAPTER 29

THE ANNUAL ACCOUNTING CONCEPT

SECTION 2. NET OPERATING LOSS CARRYOVER AND CARRYBACK

Page 1069:

After the third full paragraph, insert:

In re Harvard Industries. Inc., 568 F.3d 444 (3d Cir. 2009), involved a bankruptcy proceeding in which the taxpayer claimed income tax refunds based on carrybacks of specified liability losses. The taxpayer produced defective products. The defects did not result in any physical injuries to persons or property, but the taxpayer suffered monetary losses in suits by distributors who could not resell the defective products. The court concluded that "loss of property" in § 172(f) could refer to the loss of the defective product itself so that losses attributable to settlements with distributors who could not sell the defective product qualified under the definition of specified liability losses.

PART IX

TAX MOTIVATED TRANSACTIONS

CHAPTER 35

STATUTORY LIMITATIONS ON LEVERAGED TAX SHELTERS

SECTION 2. PASSIVE ACTIVITY LOSS LIMITATION

Page 1221:

After the carryover paragraph, insert:

3.2.1. *Application to Partners and LLC Members*

      A general partner does not qualify as material participant merely because of the partner's status as a general partner. The level of participation in each activity in which the partnership is engaged must be tested separately. A partner may be active as to some partnership activities and passive as to others.

      Section 469(h)(2) generally requires that a limited partner be treated as not materially participating in any partnership activity. The definition of a limited partner in Temp. Reg. § 1.469–5T(e)(3)(B), as a partner whose liability is limited to a fixed amount (including the partner's capital contribution), includes a member of an limited liability company (LLC), limited liability partnership (LLP), and other entities that provide all of their owners with limited liability. Temp. Reg. § 1.469-5T(e) provides two exceptions to the rule in § 469(h)(2) that a limited partner (as defined as described above) does not materially participate in a partnership activity. First, a limited partner materially participates in a partnership activity if any one of tests (1), (5), or (6) for material participation described above are met. Second, a limited partnership interest held by a general partner is not treated as a limited partnership interest in applying § 469; whether the partner materially participates is determined for the partner's aggregate interest in the partnership under the above described seven tests.

Despite the language in the temporary regulation, Garnett v. Commissioner, 132 T.C. 368 (2009), held that an interest in an LLC (or LLP or other entity in which all members receive the benefit of limited liability) is not treated as a limited partnership interest under § 469(h)(2). Thompson v. United States, 87 Fed. Cl. 728 (2009), reached the same result. Both courts reasoned that § 469(h)(2) treats limited partners differently because of an assumption that limited partners do not materially participate in their limited partnerships. Active participation in a limited partnership would cause a limited partner to lose the benefit of limited liability. In an LLC, on the other hand, all members have limited liability regardless of whether or not they participate in management. Thus, whether or not the taxpayer is a material participant requires a factual inquiry in which a taxpayer can demonstrate material participation in the activity by using any of the seven tests in Temp. Reg. § 1.469-5T(a).. The IRS has acquiesced in *Thompson*, AOD 2010-02 (March 9, 2010), and has proposed regulations that would determine limited partnership status for purposes of § 469(h)(2) by evaluating the partner's right to participate in the management of the entity. Prop. Reg. § 1.469-5(e)(3) (2011).

Page 1224:

After the second full paragraph, insert:

In Trask v. Commissioner, T.C. Memo. 2010-78, the taxpayer failed to make an explicit election on his return to aggregate rental real estate activities as required by Treas. Reg. § 1.469-9(g). The court held that merely aggregating real estate rental activity losses on his returns was not an effective election. Thus, although the taxpayer established that he was a "real estate professional" as defined in § 469(c)(7), all of the claimed losses were disallowed because he failed to prove that he materially participated any of the rental activities on an activity-by-activity basis. Rev. Proc. 2010-13, 2010-4 I.R.B. 329, requires taxpayers to report to the IRS their groupings and regroupings of activities and the addition of activities within their existing groupings of activities.

CHAPTER 36

ECONOMIC SUBSTANCE DOCTRINE

Page 1246:

After the Compaq case, before the Illustrative Material, insert:

Klamath Strategic Investment Fund v. United States
United States Court of Appeals, Fifth Circuit, 2009.
568 F.3d 537.

■ GARZA, Circuit Judge:

In this tax case, Plaintiffs Klamath Strategic Investment Fund (Klamath) and Kinabalu Strategic Investment Fund (Kinabalu) (collectively, the Partnerships) filed suit against defendant the United States of America for readjustment of partnership items. Both parties appeal various aspects of the district court's readjustment determination. For the following reasons, we affirm in part, vacate in part, and remand.

I

This case involves a highly complex series of financial transactions, which the district court categorized as a tax shelter known as Bond Linked Issue Premium Structure (BLIPS). The transactions were undertaken by two law partners, Cary Patterson and Harold Nix. Patterson and Nix's law firm represented the State of Texas in litigation against the tobacco industry and each partner earned around $30 million between 1998 and 2000. Interested in managing this wealth, Patterson and Nix requested their long-time accounting firm, Pollans & Cohen, to investigate investment opportunities.

The accountants identified Presidio Advisory Services (Presidio), an investment advisory firm purporting to specialize in foreign currency trading. Presidio advocated a complex plan involving strategic investments in foreign currencies pegged to the U.S. dollar. Patterson and Nix agreed to invest in

Presidio's plan. Generally, the Presidio strategy was structured as a three-stage, seven-year investment program. Stage I lasted 60 days and entailed relatively low risk investments. Stage II lasted from day 60 through day 180, and the risk was somewhat higher. Stage III extended from day 180 through the end of the seventh year and involved the highest risk as well as potentially the highest return. At each stage of the plan, Presidio required the investors to contribute significantly more capital. The investors retained the right to exit the plan at the end of Stage I and at each 60-day period thereafter.

To implement the strategy Presidio formed Klamath and Kinabalu as limited liability companies, taxed as partnerships. Next, Presidio formed two single-member LLCs, which are disregarded for tax purposes: St. Croix for Patterson and Rogue for Nix. Patterson owned 100% of St. Croix, and St. Croix became a 90% partner of Klamath. The other 10% partners of Klamath were Presidio Resources LLC and Presidio Growth LLC. Presidio Growth was the managing partner. Kinabalu had a similar structure. Nix owned 100% of Rogue, and Rogue was a 90% partner of Kinabalu. The other 10% partners of Kinabalu were Presidio Growth and Presidio Resources, with Presidio Growth acting as the managing partner.

To fund Klamath and Kinabalu, Patterson and Nix (acting through St. Croix and Rogue) made two distinct contributions. First, they each contributed $1.5 million to their respective partnership. Second, they entered into loan transactions with National Westminster Bank (NatWest), where the bank loaned each company $66.7 million. This included $41.7 million denominated as the "Stated Principal Amount" and $25 million as a "loan premium." The classification of the $25 million as something different than the principal loan amount is central to this case. The loan premium was given in exchange for Patterson and Nix paying NatWest a higher than market interest rate on the principal: 17.97%. To protect NatWest from the possibility that the loans would be repaid early and the benefit of the higher interest rate would not be realized, the credit agreements required that a prepayment amount be paid if the loans were paid off early. The prepayment amount would vary depending on when the loan was repaid, starting at about $25 million and decreasing over seven years. After year seven, no prepayment amount would apply.

Patterson and Nix each contributed the $66.7 million to Klamath and Kinabalu and assigned the corresponding loan obligations to the Partnerships. The Partnerships deposited the funds into accounts controlled by NatWest. Presidio directed Klamath and Kinabalu to use these funds to purchase very low risk contracts on U.S. dollars and Euros. They also made small, short 60- to 90-day term forward contract trades in foreign currencies. These were the only investments the Partnerships ever made, and Patterson and Nix elected to withdraw from Klamath and Kinabalu before the end of Stage I. They received cash and Euros on liquidation, and they sold the Euros in 2000, 2001, and 2002.

On their income tax returns for 2000, 2001, and 2002, Patterson claimed total losses of $25,277,202 arising from Klamath's activities and Nix claimed total losses of $25,272,344 arising from Kinabalu's. These massive losses occurred because each partner claimed a significant tax basis in their respective partnership. Generally, a partner's basis in a partnership is determined by the amount of capital he contributes to the partnership, and when a partnership loses money the partners can only deduct the losses from their taxable income to the extent of their basis in the partnership. When a partnership assumes a partner's individual liabilities, the liability amount is subtracted from the partner's basis. Patterson and Nix were able to report such high losses because when they each calculated their basis in the partnership, they did not reduce it by the $25 million loan premium amount. When Patterson and Nix contributed the $66.7 million plus the $1.5 million to Klamath and Kinabalu, they would have each had a $68.2 million basis in their partnership. However, the Partnerships also assumed the loan obligations, so Patterson and Nix's bases had to be reduced by the amount of the liabilities. Patterson and Nix did not consider the loan premiums to be liabilities, so they only subtracted the $41.7 million principal amount. Therefore, each claimed a taxable basis in the partnership in excess of $25 million. This meant that when Patterson and Nix sold the Euros, they were able to deduct over $25 million from their taxable income.

The IRS disagreed with this basis calculation, and in 2004 issued Final Partnership Administrative Adjustments (FPAAs) to Klamath and Kinabalu stating that under 26 U.S.C. § 752 of the Internal Revenue Code (the Code), the partners should have treated the entire $66.7 million as a liability. Alternatively, the IRS argued that the transactions were shams or lacked economic substance and should be disregarded for tax purposes. The FPAAs also made adjustments to operational expenses reported by the Partnerships and asserted accuracy-related penalties. Patterson and Nix paid the taxes owed based on the FPAAs, and then re-formed the partnerships in order to seek readjustment in the district court.

The Partnerships filed suit against the Government under 26 U.S.C. § 6226 for readjustment of partnership items.* * * [F]ollowing a bench trial the district court held that the loan transactions must nonetheless be disregarded for federal tax purposes because they lacked economic substance. The district court also concluded that * * * the Partnerships' operational expenses were deductible. * * * Finally, the court issued an order holding that * * * Patterson and Nix could deduct the $250,000 management fee paid to their accountants.

* * * The Partnerships [appeal] the district court's bench trial judgment, arguing that the loan transactions had economic substance.

III

We first consider * * * whether the district court erred in determining that the loan transactions lacked economic substance and must be disregarded for tax purposes.

The economic substance doctrine allows courts to enforce the legislative purpose of the Code by preventing taxpayers from reaping tax benefits from transactions lacking in economic reality. See Coltec Indus., Inc. v. United States, 454 F.3d 1340, 1353-54 (Fed.Cir.2006). As the Supreme Court has recognized, taxpayers have the right to decrease or avoid taxes by legally permissible means. See Gregory v. Helvering, 293 U.S. 465, 469 (1935). However, "transactions which do not vary control or change the flow of economic benefits are to be dismissed from consideration." See Higgins v. Smith, 308 U.S. 473, 476 (1940). In a more recent pronouncement, the Supreme Court held that "[w]here ... there is a genuine multiple-party transaction with economic substance which is compelled or encouraged by business or regulatory realities, is imbued with tax-independent considerations, and is not shaped solely by tax-avoidance features that have meaningless labels attached, the Government should honor the allocation of rights and duties effectuated by the parties." Frank Lyon, 435 U.S. at 583-84.

The law regarding whether a transaction should be disregarded as lacking economic reality is somewhat unsettled in the Fifth Circuit, and a split exists among other Circuits. The Fourth Circuit applies a rigid two-prong test, where a transaction will only be invalidated if it lacks economic substance and the taxpayer's sole motive is tax avoidance. See Rice's Toyota World, Inc. v. Comm'r, 752 F.2d 89, 91-92 (4th Cir.1985). The majority view, however, is that a lack of economic substance is sufficient to invalidate the transaction regardless of whether the taxpayer has motives other than tax avoidance. See, e.g., Coltec, 454 F.3d at 1355; United Parcel Serv. of Am., Inc. v. Comm'r, 254 F.3d 1014, 1018 (11th Cir.2001); ACM Partnership v. Comm'r, 157 F.3d 231, 247 (3d Cir.1998); James v. Comm'r, 899 F.2d 905, 908-09 (10th Cir.1990). We have previously declined to explicitly adopt either approach. See Compaq, 277 F.3d at 781-82 (finding that the transaction in question had both economic substance and a legitimate business purpose, so it would be recognized for tax purposes under either the minority or majority approach).

We conclude that the majority view more accurately interprets the Supreme Court's prescript in Frank Lyon. The Court essentially set up a multi-factor test for when a transaction must be honored as legitimate for tax purposes, with factors including whether the transaction (1) has economic substance compelled by business or regulatory realities, (2) is imbued with tax-independent considerations, and (3) is not shaped totally by tax-avoidance features. See Frank Lyon, 435 U.S. at 583-84. Importantly, these factors are phrased in the conjunctive, meaning that the absence of any one of them will render the transaction void for tax purposes. Thus, if a transaction lacks economic substance compelled by business or regulatory realities, the transaction must be disregarded even if the taxpayers profess a genuine business purpose without tax-avoidance motivations.

The following facts found by the district court are critical to this issue: Presidio and NatWest understood that the transactions would not last beyond Stage I, despite the purported seven-year term-meaning that the high risk foreign currency transactions were never intended to occur. If the investors failed to withdraw voluntarily, NatWest could use economic pressure to force them out because the credit agreements required the borrowers to maintain collateral on deposit at NatWest that exceeded the value of the maximum obligations owed to the bank by some varying amount. At the time the loans were issued, this amount was at least 101.25% of the total $66.7 million. NatWest had the discretion to determine whether the ratio was satisfied and could accelerate the ratio to declare a default if the bank wished to force an investor to withdraw. This requirement also meant that none of the $66.7 million loan could ever be used for investments-it had to stay in the accounts at NatWest. NatWest and Presidio understood that the bank would hold the money in relatively risk-free time deposits. Presidio's management fee was calculated as a percentage of the tax losses generated by the investment plan. The district court determined, however, that Patterson and Nix pursued the transactions with a genuine profit motive and were not solely driven by the desire to avoid taxes.

Here, the evidence supports the district court's conclusion that the loan transactions lacked economic substance. Numerous bank documents stated that despite the purported seven-year term, the loans would only be outstanding for about 70 days. NatWest's profit in the loan transactions was calculated based on a 72-day period. In the event that the investors wanted to remain with the plan beyond 72 days, NatWest would force them out. The bank noted in an internal memo that it "had no legal or moral obligation to deal [with the investors] after Day 60." During that 60- to 70-day window the loan funds could not be used to facilitate the investment strategy that Presidio designed. The requirement of keeping at least 101.25% of the $66.7 million in the NatWest account meant, as the Government's expert testified, that the Partnerships could not make any investments without supplying their own funds in excess of the loan amount.

The Partnerships contend that the loan funds were critical to the high-risk foreign currency transactions even if the funding amount could not be spent because the money provided the necessary security for the high-risk transactions. However, the structure of the plan shows that these high-risk transactions could not occur until Stage III, which was never intended to be reached. As the district court found, NatWest would force the investors out long before Stage III, so the loan transactions served no real purpose beyond creating a massive tax benefit for Nix and Patterson.

The Partnerships further argue that the loan transactions had a reasonable possibility of profit, as evidenced by the fact that two small, low-risk investments were actually made in foreign currencies. However, these investments were made using the $1.5 million that Patterson and Nix contributed to the Partnerships, not the funding amounts of the loans. Various courts have held that when applying the economic substance doctrine, the proper focus is on the particular transaction that gives rise to the tax benefit, not collateral transactions that do not produce tax benefits. See Coltec, 454 F.3d at 1356-57; Nicole Rose Corp. v. Comm'r, 320 F.3d 282, 284 (2d Cir.2002). Here, the transactions that provided the tax benefits at issue were the loans from NatWest. Therefore, the proper focus is on whether the loan transactions presented a reasonable possibility of profit, not whether the capital contributions from Patterson and Nix could have produced a profit. The loan transactions could never have been profitable because the funding amount could not actually be used for investments, and the high-risk investments for which the funding amount might have provided security were never intended to occur.

The evidence clearly shows that Presidio and NatWest designed the loan transactions and the investment strategy so that no reasonable possibility of profit existed and so that the funding amount would create massive tax benefits but would never actually be at risk. Regardless of Patterson and Nix's desire to make money, they entered into transactions controlled by Presidio and NatWest that were not structured or implemented to make a profit. This particular situation highlights the logic of following the majority approach to the economic substance doctrine, because the minority approach would allow tax benefits to flow from transactions totally lacking in economic substance as long as the taxpayers offered some conceivable profit motive. In cases such as the instant one, this approach would essentially reward a "head in the sand" defense where taxpayers can profess a profit motive but agree to a scheme structured and controlled by parties with the sole purpose of achieving tax benefits for them. We therefore agree with the district court that since the loan transactions lacked economic substance, they must be disregarded for tax purposes.

IV

***

C

The Government also appeals the district court's order that the Partnerships may deduct "operational expenses" associated with the loan and foreign currency transactions. These operational expenses include interest on the loans, a breakage fee, a management fee paid to Presidio, and a $250,000 fee paid to Pollans & Cohen. The Government argues that the district court erred because no deduction may be taken for expenses related to a sham transaction.

***

Generally, when a transaction is disregarded for lack of economic substance, deductions for costs expended in furtherance of the transaction are prohibited. See Winn-Dixie Stores, Inc. v. Comm'r, 113 T.C.254, 294 (1999) (observing that "a transaction that lacks economic substance is not recognized for Federal tax purposes" and that "denial of recognition means that such a transaction cannot be the basis for a deductible expense"); * * * This makes sense in light of the fact that the effect of disregarding a transaction for lack of economic substance is that, for taxation purposes, the transaction is viewed to have never occurred at all. * * * However, courts have upheld deductions based on genuine debts, where the debts are elements of a transaction that overall is lacking in economic substance. See Rice's Toyota World, Inc. v. Comm'r, 752 F.2d 89, 95-96 (4th Cir.1985) (allowing deductions based on recourse note debt that was an element of a sham purchase transaction, because the notes represented actual indebtedness).

Here, the district court concluded that the interest payments were deductible because they were real economic losses. However, § 163 does not base the deductibility of interest on whether or not the interest paid was a real economic loss. Rather, the test is simply whether the interest was paid or accrued on indebtedness. See Salley, 464 F.2d at 485 (disallowing interest deductions under § 163 because the taxpayers did not take on actual indebtedness: "[i]n no sense can it be said that taxpayers paid any interest . . .as compensation for the use or forbearance of money. . . which is the standard business test of indebtedness") (internal quotations and citation omitted). Further, "the fact that an enforceable debt exists between the borrower and lender is not dispositive of whether interest arising from that debt is deductible under section 163." Winn-Dixie Stores, 113 T.C. at 279. The overall transaction must have economic substance in order to show genuine indebtedness, otherwise "every tax shelter . . . could qualify for an interest expense deduction as long as there was a real creditor in the transaction that demanded repayment." Id.

In concluding that the loan transactions in this case lacked economic substance, the district court found that "[i]n truth, NatWest did not make any loans" and "[t]he loans .. . . were not loans at all." These findings preclude the conclusion that the Partnerships took on actual indebtedness. As we found above, the loan transactions in this case lacked economic substance partly because they were structured such that the Partnerships could never actually spend the loaned funds-101.25% of the funding amount had to stay in the accounts at

NatWest to prevent a default. Therefore, despite the appearance of a loan, functionally the Partnerships never took on any actual debt. Since the loans did not constitute indebtedness, the Partnerships may not deduct the interest paid under § 163.

Presumably, though not specified, the district court found the remainder of the operating expenses and fees deductible under § 212 as necessary expenses incurred. This provision requires a profit motive. See Agro Science, 934 F.2d at 576 (noting that an expenditure is deductible under § 212 "only . . . if the facts and circumstances indicate that the taxpayer made them primarily in furtherance of a bona fide profit objective independent of tax consequences"). The Government argues that the profit motive must be determined based on Presidio's subjective intentions because Presidio acted as managing partner when the transactions occurred. The district court, however, determined that the proper focus is on the motives of Patterson and Nix. Having concluded that Patterson and Nix entered into the transactions genuinely seeking to make a profit, the district court allowed the deductions.

The profit motive of a partnership is determined at the partnership level. Id.; *Simon v. Comm'r*, 830 F.2d 499, 507 (3d Cir.1987). * * * Here, the district court concluded that the partners had different motivations: Nix and Patterson at all times pursued the investment strategy with a genuine profit motive, while Presidio's primary intent was to achieve a tax benefit. The crucial inquiry, then is which partner's intentions should be attributed to the Partnership. Under Agro Science, this answer depends on which partner effectively controlled the partnership's activities. * * *

During the time of the transactions in question, Presidio acted as the managing partner but had less than 10% ownership of Klamath and Kinabalu. Patterson and Nix each had 90% ownership. * * * [T]he LLC agreements state that "the overall management and control of the business and affairs of the Company shall be vested solely in the Managing Member." The district court, however, did not analyze which partner retained control over the partnership. The district court appears to have concluded, with little explanation, that Patterson and Nix's motives must be attributed to the Partnerships because they paid the expenses at issue here and reported them on their individual tax returns. However, for purposes of determining the deductibility of expenses it is the motive of the Partnership that matters, regardless of whether certain operating expenses were borne by one partner or another. None of the arguments articulated by the Partnerships or the district court persuade us that the motives of Patterson and Nix, to whom the overall control and management of the Partnerships was expressly denied under the LLC agreements, should be attributed to the Partnerships. We therefore hold that the district court erred as a matter of law by failing to consider which partners effectively controlled the management of the Partnerships' affairs, at the time the transactions occurred, in determining whether the operating expenses and fees are deductible.

***
V

For the foregoing reasons, we AFFIRM the district court's judgment that the loan transactions lacked economic substance and must be disregarded for tax purposes. * * * We VACATE the district court's order allowing the deduction of interest and operating expenses and REMAND for reconsideration in accordance with this opinion. * * *

Pages 1249-1252:

Replace 1.2. *Proposed Codification of Economic Substance,* **with:**

1.2 Codification of Economic Substance Doctrine

The Health Care and Education Reconciliation Act of 2010 added new § 7701(o), codifying the economic substance doctrine. Codification of the economic substance doctrine has been on the legislative agenda many times since early in the first decade of this century. The move for codification was motivated in part by the insistence of not a few tax practitioners that the economic substance doctrine simply was not a legitimate element of the tax doctrine, notwithstanding its application by the courts in many cases over several decades. This argument was based on the assertion that the Supreme Court had never actually applied the economic substance doctrine to deny a taxpayer any tax benefits, conveniently pretending that the Supreme Court had never decided Knetsch v. United States, 364 U.S. 361 (1960). Congressional concern was intensified by the decision of the Court of Federal Claims in Coltec Industries, Inc. v. United States, 62 Fed. Cl. 716 (2004), which was vacated and remanded by the Federal Circuit, text page 1229. The Court of Federal Claims questioned the continuing viability of the doctrine, stating that "the use of the 'economic substance' doctrine to trump 'mere compliance with the Code' would violate the separation of powers." See STAFF OF THE JOINT COMMITTEE ON TAXATION, TECHNICAL EXPLANATION OF THE REVENUE PROVISIONS OF THE "RECONCILIATION ACT OF 2010," AS AMENDED, IN COMBINATION WITH THE "PATIENT PROTECTION AND AFFORDABLE CARE ACT," 144 (JCX-18-10, March 21, 2010) (Jt. Committee Staff). However, in that case the trial court found that the particular transaction at issue did not lack economic substance, and thus the trial court did not actually rule on its validity. On appeal, the Court of Appeals for the Federal Circuit vacated the Court of Federal Claims decision and, reiterating the validity of the economic substance doctrine, held that transaction in question lacked economic substance.

The codification of the economic substance doctrine in new § 7701(o) clarifies and standardizes some applications of the economic substance doctrine when it is applied, but does not establish any rules for determining when the doctrine should be applied. According to the legislative history, "the provision [§ 7701(o)(5)(C)] does not change present law standards in determining when to utilize an economic substance analysis." See Jt. Committee Staff, 152. Thus, "the fact that a transaction meets the requirements for specific treatment under any provision of the Code is not determinative of whether a transaction or series of transactions of which it is a part has economic substance." Id., at 153. Codification of the economic substance doctrine was not intended to alter or supplant any other judicial interpretive doctrines, such as the business purpose, substance over form, and step transaction doctrines, any similar rule in the Code, regulations, or guidance thereunder; section 7701(o) is intended merely to supplement all the other rules. Id., at 155.

One of the most important aspects of new § 7701(o) is that it requires a *conjunctive* analysis under which a transaction has economic substance only if (1) the transaction changes the taxpayer's economic position in a meaningful way apart from Federal income tax effects *and* (2) the taxpayer has a substantial business purpose, apart from Federal income tax effects, for entering into such transaction. (The second prong of most versions of the codified economic substance doctrine introduced in earlier Congresses had added "and the transaction is a reasonable means of accomplishing such purpose." See, e.g., H.R. 2345, 110th Cong, 1st Sess. (2007); H.R. 2, 108th Cong., 1st Sess. (2003). It is not clear what difference in application was intended by adoption of the different final statutory language.) This conjunctive test resolves the split between the Circuits (and between the Tax Court and certain Circuits) by rejecting the view of those courts that find the economic substance doctrine to have been satisfied if there is either (1) a change in taxpayer's economic position *or* (2) a nontax business purpose, see, e.g., Rice's Toyota World v. Commissioner, 752 F.2d 89 (4th Cir. 1985); IES Industries, Inc. v. United States, 253 F.3d 350, 353 (8th Cir. 2001). Section 7701(o)(5)(D) allows the economic substance doctrine to be applied to a single transaction or to a series of transactions. The Staff of the Joint Committee Report indicates that the provision "does not alter the court's ability to aggregate, disaggregate, or otherwise recharacterize a transaction when applying the doctrine," and gives as an example the courts' ability "to bifurcate a transaction in which independent activities with non-tax objectives are combined with an unrelated item having only tax-avoidance objectives in order to disallow those tax-motivated benefits".

Section 7701(o)(2) does not require that the taxpayer establish profit potential in order to prove that a transaction results in a meaningful change in the taxpayer's economic position or that the taxpayer has a substantial non-Federal-income-tax purpose. Nor does it specify a threshold required return if the taxpayer relies on the profit potential to try to establish economic substance. (In this respect the enacted version differs from earlier proposals that would have required the reasonably expected pre-tax profit from the transaction to exceed a risk-free rate of return. See, e.g., H.R. 2345, 110th Cong, 1st Sess. (2007); H.R. 2, 108th Cong., 1st Sess. (2003).)) But if the taxpayer does rely on a profit potential claim, then the profit potential requires a present value analysis:

The potential for profit of a transaction shall be taken into account in determining whether the requirements of [the § 7701(o) test for economic substance] are met with respect to the transaction only if the present value of the reasonably expected pre-tax profit from the transaction is substantial in relation to the present value of the expected net tax benefits that would be allowed if the transaction were respected. Jt. Committee Staff, 154-55.

Thus the analysis of profit potential by the Court of Federal Claims in Consolidated Edison Co. of New York v. United States, 90 Fed. Cl. 228 (2009), which appears not to have thoroughly taken into account present value analysis, would not stand muster under the new provision. In all events, transaction costs must be taken into account in determining pre-tax profits, and the statute authorizes regulations requiring foreign taxes to be treated as expenses in determining pre-tax profit in appropriate cases. Any State or local income tax effect that is related to a Federal income tax effect is treated in the same manner as a Federal income tax effect. Thus, state tax savings that piggy-back on Federal income tax savings cannot provide either a profit potential or a business purpose. Similarly, a financial accounting benefit cannot satisfy the business purpose requirement if the financial accounting benefit originates in a reduction of Federal income tax.

Section 7701(o)(5)(B) specifically provides that the statutory modifications and clarifications apply to an individual only with respect to "transactions entered into in connection with a trade or business or an activity engaged in for the production of income." More importantly, according to the Jt. Committee Staff, 152-153, "[The provision is not intended to alter the tax treatment of certain basic business transactions that, under longstanding judicial and administrative practice are respected, merely because the choice between meaningful economic alternatives is largely or entirely based on comparative tax advantages." The list of transactions and decisions intended to be immunized for the application of the economic substance doctrine includes: (1) the choice between capitalizing a business enterprise with debt or equity; (2) a U.S. person's choice between utilizing a foreign corporation or a domestic corporation to make a foreign investment; (3) the choice to enter a transaction or series of transactions that constitute a corporate organization or reorganization under subchapter C;

and (4) the choice to utilize a related-party entity in a transaction, provided that the arm's length standard of section 482 and other applicable concepts are satisfied.

Leasing transactions will continue to be scrutinized based on all of the facts and circumstances.

Many earlier versions of the codification of economic substance doctrine, some of which were adopted by the House, also provided special rules for applying what was essentially a *per se* lack of economic substance in transactions with tax indifferent parties that involved financing, and artificial income and basis shifting. See, e.g., H.R. 2345, 110th Cong, 1st Sess. (2007); H.R. 2, 108th Cong., 1st Sess. (2003). These rules did not make it into the enacted version. Special statutory rules for determining the profitability of leasing transactions also did not find their way into the final statutory enactment.

New § 6662(b)(6), in conjunction with new § 6664(c)(2), imposes a strict liability 20 percent penalty for an underpayment attributable to any disallowance of claimed tax benefits by reason of a transaction lacking economic substance, within the meaning of new § 7701(o), "or failing to meet the requirements of any similar rule of law." The penalty is increased to 40 percent if the taxpayer does not adequately disclose the relevant facts on the original return or an amended return filed before the taxpayer has been contacted for audit — an amended return filed after that time cannot cure original sin. I.R.C. § 6664(i). Because the § 6664(c) "reasonable cause" exception is unavailable, outside (or in-house) analysis and opinions of counsel or other tax advisors will not insulate a taxpayer from the penalty if a transaction is found to lack economic substance. Likewise, new § 6664(d)(2) precludes a reasonable cause defense to imposition of the § 6662A reportable transaction understatement penalty for a transaction that lacks economic substance. (Section § 6662A(e)(2) has been amended to provide that the § 6662A penalty with respect to a reportable transaction understatement does not apply to a transaction that lacks economic substance if a 40 percent penalty is imposed under § 6662(i)). A similar no-fault penalty regime applies to excessive erroneous refund claims that are denied on the ground that the transaction on which the refund claim was based lacked economic substance. I.R.C. § 6676(c).

CHAPTER 36 ECONOMIC SUBSTANCE DOCTRINE

Page 1262:

After the last paragraph, insert:

In New Phoenix Sunrise Corporation v. Commissioner, 132 T.C. 161 (2009), the taxpayer entered into a tax shelter (called a BLISS transaction) that involved the purchase of two pairs of option contracts in a transaction designed to eliminate $10 million of capital gain realized on the sale of some assets. The long portion of the options was purchased from Deutsche Bank AG for an initial payment of $10.631 million plus two additional payments of $63 million each. The short option was sold to Deutsche Bank for an initial payment of $10.369 million and two additional payments of $63.066 million. Only the $138,750 difference between the purchase and sales prices changed hands. The options called for offsetting payments based on the U.S. $/Japanese ¥ price with a variance in the options of only 0.00002 (2 Pips). The taxpayer contributed the purchased and sold options to a general partnership for a 99% interest. The 1% partner was a dominant shareholder in the taxpayer. The taxpayer claimed a basis in its partnership interest in the amount of the cost of the purchased long option. It also claimed that its liability on the short position of the sold option was a contingent liability that did not reduce the basis in its partnership interest. Thereafter, the partnership acquired shares of Cisco stock for $149,958. After the options expired, the partnership distributed the Cisco stock to the taxpayer, and the taxpayer claimed that pursuant to § 732 it had a basis in the Cisco stock equal to its partnership interest basis, and as a result realized a $10 million loss on its subsequent sale of the Cisco stock. The court rejected the claimed loss on several grounds. First, the taxpayer did not suffer a real economic loss. "The loss claimed as a result of the stepped-up basis in the Cisco stock was purely fictional." Second, the transaction had no realistic possibility of earning a profit. Deutsche Bank's control as the calculation agent for the option contracts empowered it to assure that the market rate chosen for the closing of the options would never trigger the so-called "sweet spot" under which the investor would earn substantial profits. Third, the transaction lacked economic substance. The court stated:

> Absent the benefit of the claimed tax loss, there was nothing but a cash flow that was negative for all relevant periods—the "hallmark" of an economic sham as the Court of Appeals for the Sixth Circuit has held. Dow Chem. Co. v. United States, 435 F.3d at 602 (quoting Am. Elec. Power Co. v. United States, 326 F.3d 737, 742 (6th Cir. 2003). Such a deal lacks economic substance. Id. Because we find that the transaction at issue lacked economic substance, we do not consider Mr. Wray's and Capital's profit motive in entering into the transaction. Id. at 605; . . . Pursuant to the aforementioned cases, the BLISS transaction must be ignored for Federal income tax purposes. Accordingly, the

overstated loss claimed as a result of the sale of the Cisco stock is disregarded, as is the flowthrough loss from Olentangy Partners.

The court disallowed a $500,000 deduction for fees paid to a law firm for the tax opinion and structuring the transaction, because the fees were not incurred in the production of any income against which a deduction is allowable

The court also sustained a 40 percent gross valuation penalty under § 6662(e) and (h), holding that the undervaluation penalty is applicable to overstated basis. The court indicated that the § 6662(d) substantial understatement of tax and the § 6662(c) negligence penalties were applicable. However, because the penalties are not additive, only the gross valuation penalty was imposed. The court rejected the taxpayer's argument that it reasonably relied on the attorney's tax shelter opinion.

PART X

THE TAXABLE UNIT

CHAPTER 37

SHIFTING INCOME AMONG TAXABLE UNITS

SECTION 1. INCOME FROM PERSONAL SERVICES

Page 1265:

After the first full paragraph, insert:

The Poe v. Seaborn rule has recently sprung back to life in the context of same-sex relationships that are legally recognized in states that have community property laws. Because of the federal Defense of Marriage Act (discussed at page 1311 of the text), same-sex relationships are never recognized as marriages for federal tax purposes regardless of how they are characterized under state law. Nevertheless, under the law of certain states, formally recognized same-sex relationships trigger community property rules. As a result, the IRS has ruled that registered domestic partners (RDPs) in California (a community property state) must each report on their own individual returns one-half of the combined income from both partners' performance of services and one-half of the combined income derived from the partners' community property assets. P.L.R. 201021048. This income-splitting means that RDPs in California generally receive more favorable tax results than people who are, under federal law, considered married and can be subjected to the so-called "marriage penalty" (discussed in the text at page 1307). While the IRS ruling involved a California RDP, the same rule would apply to RDPs in Nevada and Washington (both of which, like California, have both registered domestic partnership laws and community property laws) and to California same-sex marriages that took place during the time period when those marriages were legally permissible in that state.

PART XI

Alternative Minimum Tax

CHAPTER 39

Alternative Minimum Tax for Individuals

Section 1. Structure of the AMT

Page 1352:

At the end of the carryover paragraph, add:

Since publication of the text, Congress annually has temporarily increased the exemption amounts (for 2011, to $74,450 for joint returns and $48,450 for unmarried individuals). At the time this supplement went to press, Congress had not yet increased the exemption amounts for 2012.

PART X ALTERNATIVE MINIMUM TAX

Page 1356:

At the end of the carryover paragraph, add:

Congress extended the ability to use the specified personal nonrefundable credits to reduce AMT liability until December 31, 2011. It is possible that Congress will retroactively extend this rule, though it had not yet done so at the time this supplement went to press.